MANPOWER
FOR ENERGY PRODUCTION

MANPOWER FOR ENERGY PRODUCTION

An International Guide to Sources with Annotations

Compiled by
Djehane A. Hosni

Bibliographies and Indexes in Economics and Economic History, Number 5

GREENWOOD PRESS
New York • Westport, Connecticut • London

LIBRARY OF CONGRESS CATALOGING-IN-PUBLICATION DATA

Hosni, Djehane A.
  Manpower for energy production.

  (Bibliographies and indexes in economics and
economic history, ISSN 0749-1786 ; no. 5)
  Bibliography: p.
  Includes index.
  1. Energy industries—Employees—Supply and demand—
Bibliography. I. Title. II. Series.
Z7164.L1H67   1986   016.33112'921042   86-19377
[HD8039.E47]
ISBN 0-313-25089-8 (lib. bdg. : alk. paper)

Library of Congress Catalog Card Number: 86-19377
ISBN: 0-313-25089-8
ISSN: 0749-1786

First published in 1986

Greenwood Press, Inc.
88 Post Road West, Westport, Connecticut 06881

Printed in the United States of America

∞

The paper used in this book complies with the
Permanent Paper Standard issued by the National
Information Standards Organization (Z39.48-1984).

10 9 8 7 6 5 4 3 2 1

Contents

Acknowledgments

The author wishes to express her appreciation to the University of Central Florida College of Business Administration and Library for their assistance. Special recognition is extended to the Kuwait Institute for Scientific Research and its Technoeconomics Division under whose auspices the initial research was undertaken.

The author is indebted to Mrs. Susan Vargo for her coordination and organizational efforts. Sincere appreciation is also extended to Mrs. Khadiji El. Dashti for her help with the Arabic material. Finally the author is extremely grateful to the typing efforts of Mrs. Ceceile Lindo and the word processing team, who made this manuscript a reality.

Introduction

Both developed and developing countries have been affected by the energy crisis that began in the seventies. This energy shortage triggered much debate over the last decade and generated copious literature on the subject. This publication marks the end of this phase of the energy era, signalled by the recent drop in the prices of oil.

Manpower analysis and planning is a cornerstone for the successful implementation of a national energy program. In most studies, however, the human resources aspect of the energy problems did not receive due attention. The analyses of the manpower dimension in the energy sector are scanty, results of piecemeal efforts that lack coordination. There was a definite need to review the research work completed on the subject matter and to document the different manpower energy strategies.

The energy crisis revealed the interdependence of the world economy. Accordingly, this bibliography is not confined to the U.S. economy, but provides an international perspective by drawing on the energy experiences of fifty other countries, including those of the Arab world, where both energy and manpower are critical to future economic development.

OVERVIEW

The need for energy is the force shaping our times. Imported oil is critical to U.S. economy activity. In the seventies, the focus was on sharply rising oil prices. In the mid-eighties, economists are trying to predict and analyze the impact of declining oil prices. The major developments surrounding the energy problem can be categorized into three phases. The first phase consisted of a fourfold increase in the price of oil to $12 per barrel between 1973 and 1979. The second phase ushered the threefold increase in petroleum to $35 a barrel. By 1982, the downward trend began. The lowest point of the third phase came in 1986 when the price of oil per barrel fell below $10, but the price rose again then, almost to the $15 mark. These erratic changes in prices have influenced detrimentally the economies of the world. The earlier price shocks precipitated two recessions in the United States, and severely constrained the poverty alleviation and employment generation efforts of the developing countries. With an oil import bill of over 50 percent of total imports, the buildup of these countries' prod-

uctive capacity slowed down. The adjustment process was difficult,
with many painful sacrifices. The resultant message was clear: tap
domestic energy supplies, and develop renewable energy sources.

The latest low oil prices point toward more reliance on imported
oil for the United States. At present, the cost of domestic oil production exceeds that of oil on the world market. Consequently, operating
wells are closing down in the energy-belt states, shooting unemployment
up and generating negative secondary effects throughout the oil producing economies. Yet, at the aggregate level, the picture is rosy, with
the cost of living and interest rates down, the amount of construction
up, and a break in the trade deficit. For the oil exporting countries,
declining oil revenues have negative effects on their young economies,
which are predominantly oil-dependent. Sheikh Yamani of Saudi Arabia in
a May interview on ABC Nightline warned against the long-term danger of
low oil prices, which has yet to be carefully assessed.

A comprehensive look at the energy problem under the first
scenario-that of rising prices – encompassed a wide spectrum of issues:
jobs, the environment, balance of payments, economic growth, inflation
and so forth. Three basic points need to be raised in relation to these
issues. First, energy is basic to our production and consumption needs.
Second, both the sources and uses of energy are a function of its
prices, which are very difficult to predict. Third, manpower is essential to the production and development of energy. The interest of this
text is to capitalize on the third point within the context of the
previous two. Although the share of the labor force employed in industries that engage in the production and distribution of energy is
relatively small (e.g., three percent in the U.S.), changes in the
availability of different energy sources significantly affect manpower
utilization and the demand for workers with appropriate skills.

In this book, energy production is defined in a broad sense to
include the energy-producing sector of the economy, as well as energy-
related activities. The energy-producing sector includes exploration,
facility construction, extraction, processing, transportation and other
ancillary activities.[1] Both established (e.g., oil and gas) and
emerging (e.g., solar, geothermal) energy industries are incorporated.
Energy-related activities include research and development, particularly
for those new sources of energy still at the planning stage, environmental control, and the academic programs of the education institutions
that develop the needed manpower. Both the demand for and supply of
manpower are examined. Although the main focus is on basic or direct
employment (i.e., the numbers and skills of workers involved in energy
production), secondary or indirect employment is also accounted for.
This represents the additional employment created through the energy
sector need for inputs from other industries and the consumption
expenditures of the energy workers.[2]

The energy-manpower interface in the literature is examined in the
context of economic, demographic and technological considerations. The
studies covered could be grouped into three categories. The first
category stresses the interdependence between the energy industries and
the aggregate economy. It is maintained that GNP growth, energy use,
and employment are interrelated, but that the casual relationship is not
clearly defined. The second group tackles the energy industries. As
production expands, additional labor is needed. Energy-production
details affect the estimation of energy manpower requirements. Energy-

employment models would identify the supply and demand imbalances.   The
proliferation of modelling efforts has generated a wide range of manpower estimates.   The third category of studies addresses the nature of
the individual energy subsectors (e.g., coal mining, electricity, solar
energy).   One finding, for instance, describes the future coal mining
work force as younger, better educated, and relatively immobile.
    In general the literature discusses several issues:
    1.   The substitution/complementarity of capital, labor, and energy.
    2.   The impact of changes in energy supply prices on demand, prod-
uction, and manpower requirements, taking into account the corresponding
occupational and geographic shifts.
    3.   The assessment of the energy education/training programs that
ensure the steady availability of trained manpower.
    4.   The effects of conservation and alternative energy development
on employment.
    A brief glance at the highlights of the major findings in the
literature is offered in the bibliography.   The conventional energy
industries are highly capital-intensive and require a relatively more
skilled work force.   The manpower structure associated with oil and gas,
for instance, shows a higher mix of engineers and blue-collar workers
(as craftsmen and operators) that require considerable lead time in
education and training.   Technological changes in energy production
alter the occupational composition of those employed in its ranks.   This
literature discloses the difficulty of manpower planning, which is
accomplished by estimating the demand for labor and comparing it with
the supply of labor, in order to determine the energy manpower and
training needs.   It is important, therefore, to assess the different
energy education/training programs and to strengthen the linkages
between industry and academia.   Opportunities for women, minorities,
youth, and the structurally unemployed need to be evaluated.   Efforts
need to be made to enhance women's prospects in energy-related
occupations.   Conservation and renewable energy offer viable
opportunities for the structurally unemployed.   The skills and training
requirements of solar technology are not very demanding.   Those debating
for solar energy in the solar-nuclear controversy capitalize on the job
creation potential of solar energy.   Solar technology would create three
times as many jobs as the nuclear option, and is supported by the union
leadership.
    In developing countries, the constraint of qualified managerial and
technological expertise seriously limit the planning, undertaking, and
management of the entire energy sector.   There is a great need for joint
cooperation to overcome such limitations especially in the Arab world.
    Energy development projects are massive undertakings.   Hence, their
socioeconomic impacts cannot go unnoticed.   The complexities of a
"boomtown" are well-documented.   It is important always to plan for the
participation and training of local workers.   The Environmentalists for
Full Employment (EFFE) argue that there is no trade-off between the
protection of the environment and the achievement of full employment and
hence strongly recommend the solar option.[3]
    Given the uncertainties surrounding the world of energy and the
vulnerability of the U.S. economy, recommendations for oil interruption
contingency plans are made.   There is also a general concensus on the
need for the development of an energy manpower information system in
support of energy manpower planning.

USER'S GUIDE

The table of contents provides the user with an outline of the basic energy manpower issues under discussion. The objective is to develop a methodological framework of analysis, delineating the topical areas of research. The outline identifies the energy manpower areas where information is lacking. Hopefully this will instigate further thought and inquiry into the subject matter. Many citations could possibly fall under more than one topic, but no cross-referencing is used. Each citation is entered under the topic of main concern. For each topic, entries are arranged in alphabetical order by author.

The entries include books, journal articles, government articles, reports by research firms and universities, as well as publications of international organizations. The bibliography is international in scope. It focuses on a large number of countries in addition to the United States and makes a special reference to the Arab world. The appendix provides a classification by country reflecting geographic location, income level, and trading oil status. For the United States, a regional distribution is also offered for those states under examination. The coverage extends from the oil crisis to the present time, incorporating the oil price plunge and the recent nuclear accident in the Soviet Union.

Different sources were used to identify the bibliographic entries. The DIALOG computer information service was searched. Examples of sources found through this service include Energy Line and National Technical Information Service (NTIS). In addition, two other data bases were used: RLIN (Research Libraries Information Network), which is the bibliographic data base of RLG (Research Library Group), and OCLC (Online Computer Library Center, Inc.), which represents the most widely used bibliographic database.

The following notations, found at the end of some of the annotations, indicate the granting of authorizations whenever the abstracts were taken from another source:

BC	Reprinted by permission of Bechtel Corporation
BPA	Reprinted by permission of Bonneville Power Administration
GWR	Reprinted by permission of Gower Publishing Company
IAEA	Reprinted by permission of International Atomic Energy Agency
ILO	Reprinted by permission of International Labor Organization
JHR	Reprinted by permission of the Journal of Human Resources
NHP	Reprinted by permission of North-Holland Publishing Company
NTIS	Reprinted by permission of the National Technical Information Service, U.S. Department of Commerce
AOPEC	Reprinted by permission of Arab Organization for Petroleum Exporting Countries
ORAU	Reprinted by permission of Oak Ridge Associated Universities
PPL	Reprinted by permission of Pergamon Press, Ltd.
SERI	Reprinted by permission of Solar Energy Research Institute
WB	Reprinted by permission of World Bank

Some entries were originally written in a foreign language. This was mostly the case with the Arabic material frequently referenced in the citations. Several Arabic citations come from the Proceedings of the Annual Arab Energy Conferences, sponsored by the Organization for Arab Petroleum Exporting Countries (OAPEC), in order to provide the most up-to-date information.

Entries were also included that did not address energy manpower per se, but were deemed appropriate to report on those energy changes that would ultimately affect energy manpower. Finally, to facilitate the user's task, an Author Index and Abbreviation list are provided.

NOTES:

[1]Willis J. Nordlund and R. Thayne Robson, Energy and Employment (New York: Praeger Publishers, 1980), p. 2.

[2]D. Hosni and I. Sirageldin, A Conceptual Framework for Estimating Labor Demand in the Energy Sector of the Arab Countries (Safat, Kuwait: Kuwait Institute for Scientific Research, 1985), p. 7.

[3]Richard Grossman and Gail Daneka, Guide to Jobs and Energy (Washington, D. C.: EFFE, 1977).

Abbreviations

ADB	Asian Development Bank
AFL-CIO	American Federation of Labor and Congress of Industrial Organization
AGCC	Arab Gulf Cooperation Council
ALO	Arab Labor Organization
ANS	American Nuclear Society
APAE	Administration for Planning Analysis and Evaluation
ASEE	American Society for Engineering Education
AT	Appropriate Technology
CAC	Center for Advanced Computation (Illinois)
CAITS	Center for Alternative Industrial and Technological Systems
CARE	Conservation and Renewable Energy
CEMIS	Comprehensive Energy Manpower Information System
CEP	Council on Economic Priorities
CETA	Comprehensive Employment and Training Act
CICEC	Central Illinois Consumer Energy Council
CMDS	Construction Manpower Demand System
CMHSA	Coal Mine Health and Safety Act
CRD	Committee on Energy Research and Development
CROS	Crude and Refined Oil Sector
CVTA	Central Vocational Training Administration
DHW	Domestic Hot Water
DMC	Developing Member Country
DOE	U. S. Department of Energy
DOL	U.S. Department of Labor
DRI	Data Resources, Inc.
EDF	Electricite de France
EDIO	Energy Disaggregated Input-Output Model
EEC	European Economic Community
EFFE	Environmentalists for Full Employment
E/GDP	Energy/Gross Domestic Product Ratio
EJ	Exajoules
ERDA	The Energy Research and Development Administration
ERLC	Environmental Research and Learning Center
ESPM	Energy Supply Planning Model

FEA	Federal Energy Administration
GOCO	Government-owned Contractor-operated
GNP	Gross National Product
GPO	Government Printing Office
GW	Gigawatt
HUD	Housing and Urban Development
HVAC	Heating, Ventilation and Air Conditioning
HYSOLAR	Solar Hydrogen Production and Utilization
I/O	Input/Output
IAEA	International Atomic Energy Agency
IBEW	International Brotherhood of Electrical Workers
IEA	International Energy Agency
ILO	International Labor Organization
KFAS	Kuwait Foundation for Advancement of Sciences
KISR	Kuwait Institute for Scientific Research
LNG	Liquefied Natural Gas
MW	Megawatt
Mboe/2	Million barrels per day of oil equivalent
Mtoe	Million toe
NAHB	National Association of Home Builders
NEAS	National Energy Accounting System
NRC	Nuclear Regulatory Commission
NSF	National Science Foundation
OAPEC	Organization of Arab Petroleum Exporting Countries
OCAW	Oil, Chemical and Atomic Workers' International Union
OECD	Organization for Economic Cooperation and Development
OIC	Opportunities Industrialization Center
OLADE	Latin American Energy Organization
ORAU	Oak Ridge Associated Universities
PAEC	Philippine Atomic Energy Commission
PIES	Project Independence Evaluation System
PLACE	Latin American Energy Cooperation Program
R&D	Research and Development
R/P	Reserve to Production ratio
RD&D	Research Development and Demonstration
READ	Regional Energy, Activity and Demographic (model)
RES	Regional Energy Survey
SANCST	Saudi Arabia National Center for Science and Technology
SAM	Spatial Allocation Model
SEAM	Social Economic Assessment Model
SEED	Structural Econometric Energy Demand (model)
SEIS	Solar Energy Information Services
SERI	Solar Energy Research Institute
SH	Space Heating
SMWIA	Sheet Metal Workers International Association
SRI	Stanford Research Institute
STP	Scientific and Technical Personnel
SUEDE	Solar Utilization/Economic Development and Employment Program
TER	Total primary energy requirement
TVA	Tennessee Valley Authority
UCLA	University of California at Los Angeles
UKAEA	United Kingdom Atomic Energy Association

UMW	United Mine Workers
UNCTAD	United Nations Conference on Trade and Development
UNECWA	United Nations Economic Commission for Western Asia
WAP	Weatherization Assistance Program
WEP	Working Group on Energy Policy
WINB	Western Interstate Nuclear Board
n.d.	no date

BIBLIOGRAPHY

1
Energy and the Economy

1. Abo Saffara, Hassan. "The Role of Energy in Arab Development and Economic Integration," Proceedings of Second Arab Energy Conference in Doha, Qatar, March 1982. Kuwait: OAPEC, pp. 173-203. (in Arabic)

The gravity of the energy situation at Arab and international levels is addressed. The paper discusses the critical time factor in the realization of development and Arab economic integration through the optimal utilization of Arab energy resources as fuel for energy needs, feedstock for petrochemical industries and as a source of revenues to finance economic investments to explore new petroleum reserves, to increase oil recovery and to develop alternative energy sources. The internal and external challenges confronting energy and the need for joint Arab cooperation are outlined. It also proposes the establishment of a dynamic Arab energy model for integrated development based on the joint Arab Economic Action Strategy.

2. Al-Ali, Hashim M. and Sivaciyan, Sevan. The Oil Sector in the Saudi Economy in the Mid-1970s: An Interindustrial Approach," The Journal of Energy and Development, Vol. 6, No. 1, Autumn 1980, pp. 109-120.

The purpose of this article is to focus on the crude and refined oil sector (CROS) as a sector of productive activity in Saudi Arabia and its relationship to the rest of the economy (over and above the financial link). The article examines the interindustrial allocation of CROS output first. It calculates the proportion of CROS output (2.93%) delivered directly to each sector of economic activity (27 sectors) as well as to each component (12) of final demand (97.07%). The highest proportions go to exports (91.8%), to private consumption (4.11%), government consumption (0.92%), and for capital formation in CROS (0.29%). The main direct and indirect customer sectors of CROS are identified for producing the final demand output of each sector. Construction, transport, agriculture, repair services, trade, and electricity were the main customers of CROS in the mid-seventies. The interindustrial employment relationships of CROS are assessed. CROS, being highly capital-intensive, has a low level of employment.

CROS employees are predominantly nationals. Both direct and indirect employment is examined. The ratio of indirect to direct employment was calculated as 0.32 indicating that for each 100 workers employed in CROS, an additional 32 were employed to satisfy the intermediate demand by customer sectors. The highest indirect employment effect was associated with electricity. The relationship between the interindustrial structure of CROS output and employment is made. The indirect employment effects of individual sectors are small/negligible because of its highly capital-intensive nature and low level of intermediate demand for CROS output. Total employment in CROS in 1976 represented 2.6% of non-agricultural employment. The weight of direct and indirect manpower requirements remains marginal to the total requirements of the economy. Yet, the interindustrial output and employment relationship make CROS an integral part of the domestic economy (mainly through refined products). The occupational structure of CROS indicates a high concentration of professional and skilled manpower. The specific manpower requirements of CROS are oriented towards high-level manpower. CROS is also a pioneer of vocational training programs.

3. Al-Moussa, Ali. "The Labor Force in Manufacturing," Proceedings of a Conference on Manufacturing in Kuwait. Dec. 10, 11, 26, 1983. Kuwait: Kuwait Foundation for Advancement of Sciences (KFAS), 1984. (in Arabic)

This study examines the contribution of the manufacturing sector in the national economy in terms of its share of gross domestic product (GDP) and its role in job creation. It reviews the characteristics of the workforce engaged in that sector and emphasizes the declining trend of nationals in that sector from 19.2 percent in 1975 to 7.7 percent in 1980. The labor force share of the oil sector in refineries and petrochemicals was estimated to be 19 percent of the total workforce. It houses approximately 60 percent of all nationals working in the manufacturing sector. There is a definite need for more national participation in that sector at all levels of skills that would reflect on the education and training systems of the country.

4. Allen, Edward L. and Edmonds, James A. Exogenous (Nonprice) Factors Influencing E/GNP Relationships in Leading OECD Countries. Washington, D.C.: ORAU, Institute for Energy Analysis, December 1979. ORAU/IEA-79-19(M)

This study addresses the effect of major trends other than prices on the energy demand and the energy/gross national product ratio (E/GNP) for six leading countries of the Organization for Economic Cooperation and Development (OECD)—Canada, France, Italy, Japan, the United Kingdom, and West Germany. Demographic, technological, political, and economic factors are analyzed in each country and then compared in a summary, integrated chapter.

Demographic trends had the most important influence on energy demand. In each country studied, fertility rates have fallen markedly over the past two decades and now hover around 1.8, well below the population replacement level. We expect this to continue through the remainder of this century. The consequences of low fertility rates include: (1) an increase in the participation of women in the labor force; (2) an increase in the number of female automobile drivers; and (3) a decrease in projected total labor force growth rates. In addition, the lower rate of household formation implicit in this declining population growth decreases residential energy use relative to GNP.

Industry represents the largest energy-consuming sector. Industrial energy use is expected to continue a long-term downward trend relative to GNP, even in the absence of energy price increases. (ORAU)

5.   Berg, Mark R.; Ray, Paul H.; and Boroush, Mark A.   Jobs and Energy in Michigan: The Next Twenty Years.   Ann Arbor, Michigan: The Institute for Social Research, The University of Michigan, 1981.

This expensive one-year study provides a preliminary analysis of the potential risks to Michigan's employment level which occurred because of the changes in the price and availability of energy. The study further explores the impact expected through the year 2000, particularly, if Michigan's energy policy remains unchanged.

Michigan is the most vulnerable state in the nation in terms of energy-based problems. This is a direct result of their dependence on the auto industry and durables manufacturing. It is expected that this vulnerability will increase in the future.

This study examines: 1) how energy is used and how it is related to state jobs, 2) the nature of the relationship between jobs and various types of energy problems both now and over the next 20 years, 3) the future alternatives available, 4) which types of energy supplies provide the greatest risks and opportunities of the next two decades, and 5) what major energy problems need to be addressed by the citizens, businesses and governments of Michigan.

The main conclusion of this study is that all parties will have to take strong initiatives in conservation and energy policy if Michigan's four million workers are to cope with the energy problems prevalent in an era of expensive and supply limited energy.

6.   Berndt, Ernst R. and Wood, David O.   "Technology, Prices and the Derived Demand for Energy, "Review of Economics and Statistics, Vol. 57, No. 3, August 1975, pp. 259-268.

This article provides empirical evidence on the possibilities for substitution between energy and nonenergy inputs in an effort to more clearly define the structure of manufacturing technology in the United States between 1947 and 1971. The principal finding is that technological possibilities for substitution between energy and non-energy inputs are present to a limited extent. The study shows that energy demand is price responsive, energy and labor are slightly substitutable, and energy and capital are complementary.

Implications of these results mean that the lifting of price ceilings on energy would tend to reduce the energy and capital intensiveness and increase labor intensiveness at a given level of output. Also, investment incentives generate an increased demand for capital and energy. Therefore, general investment incentives become less attractive as fiscal stimulants when energy conservation is a conscious policy goal.

7.   Bullard, Clark W. "Energy and Jobs." Paper presented at University of Michigan Conference on Energy Conservation - Path to Progress or Poverty? Ann Arbor, Michigan, November 1-2, 1977.

The study discusses the myths associated with the negative impact of energy conservation on economic growth and employment (number of jobs and the quality of work experience). This is because conservation is confused with curtailment. A dollar spent on energy creates fewer jobs than a dollar spent on most other goods and services. So energy conservation will have a favorable impact on employment. Energy saving policies to increase employment must be targeted at specific sectors. Energy conservation can create jobs that are more satisfying and fulfilling than the ones it eliminates. For the manufacture of durable goods, it would result in fewer assembly line jobs and more maintenance and repairs. The study took a closer look at the requirements for various categories of scientific and technical personnel relative to available supply for energy supply development. The results indicated no significant shortages of scientific and technical personnel at present but the demand would grow at 3 percent per year for scientists engineers and technicians throughout the economy. This 3 percent growth rate raises concern. About 11 percent of the nation's scientific and technical personnel would be associated directly and indirectly with production, processing and transportation of energy. Energy supply technologies in contrast to energy conserving technologies tend to be large and centralized and located by the energy resources. Problems of relocation and boom-town would result. This long-run impact of technological change on manpower requirements is one of uncertainty. It is recommended, therefore, to concentrate on short-term analyses of the present energy and employment situation and cultivate a feeling about the development of particular technologies tempered by an awareness of the skill composition of the workforce.

8.   Caramanis, Michael C. "Capital, Energy and Labor Cross-Substitution Elasticities in a Developing Country: The Case of Greek Manufacturing," in B.A. Bayraktar; E. A. Cherniavsky; M.A. Laughton; and Ruff, L.E. (editors). Energy Policy Planning. New York and London: Plenum Press in cooperation with NATO Scientific Affairs Division, 1981, pp. 307-316.

Greece, like many oil-importing countries in 1973 and 1974, was faced with the challenge of maintaining economic stability during inflationary times due to sizeable and abrupt increases in petroleum costs. The government policy makers identified the need to accelerate the shift toward an "optimal" mix of productive factors, especially to substitute energy with other inputs.

Two instruments were utilized. First, the long practiced policy of subsidies to manufacturers in the form of cheap energy was replaced by the policy of reflecting the real costs in private sector pricing including the cost of the imported oil. Second, the government encouraged energy-saving investment through incentives.

This study attempts to evaluate this Greek policy by analyzing the ability of the country's manufacturing to respond to it. The past short-run, cross-factor elasticities of substitution and price elasticities of demand were investigated.

The translog cost function that was employed suggested capital-labor and capital-energy substitution were mostly inelastic. Labor-energy substitution, however, was shown to be high and have economies of scale that were capital-using, labor-saving and energy-neutral. This fact indicates that government policy should remove labor constraints from the tight labor market in this country in order for energy consumption to decline.

9. Choucri, Nazli and Supriya, Lahiri. "Short-Run Energy-Economy Interaction in Egypt," World Development, Vol. 12, No. 8, 1984, pp. 799-820.

The effects of increases in the domestic oil prices on the Egyptian economy are analyzed in the framework of a short-run macro- economic model. The structural of energy-economy short-run interactions depends on the critical role that petroleum plays in relation to the consumption basket and as a factor of production. A ten sector macro-economic model is developed to examine the short-run adjustment problems. Several macro responses are evaluated; these represent effects on sectoral output, sectoral prices, income shares, and balance of payments. The analysis indicates that 1) an increase in the domestic price of oil will reduce petroleum use and prompt conservation, 2) higher inflation, drop in the share of wage income and output losses, 3) the impact of energy demand management through appropriate petroleum pricing strategy would be mitigated unless institutional and structural constraints are carefully taken into account to alleviate the cost pressures imposed by other energy sectors. Finally, it is emphasized the macroeconomic implications of domestic petroleum pricing strategies in Egypt should be carefully considered. It is very important to integrate the energy sector into the overall economy strategy.

10. Cohen, Laurie P. "Hard Times: Plunge in Oil Prices Brings Woes to Energy-Belt States," Wall Street Journal, Vol. CCVII, No. 24, February 4, 1986, pp. 1 and 23.

The impact of the drop in energy prices on the energy heartland (Oklahoma, Louisiana, Texas, Kansas, Colorado, Wyoming, and North Dakota) is discussed. The oil price skid promises renewed economic hardship. Thousands of additional persons employed by energy concerns are likely to lose their jobs as companies adjust to the price decline. The Atlantic Richfield company has plans to lay-off as many as 2,000 workers over the next year mostly in Texas, Colorado, and Wyoming. Texas alone is expected to lose 56,000 jobs. A new wave of bankruptcy filing is expected. Texas stands to lose 28,000 jobs for each $1 drop in the price of oil, reflecting its position as the No. 1 oil producer in the United States. This will have secondary effects on other parts of the economy and,

in some states, the unemployment rate might rise to double digit
figure.   These states are trying very hard to diversify their
economies.

11.   Congress of the United States.   Subcommittee on Energy of the Joint
Economic Committee.   Creating Jobs Through Energy Policy.   Washington,
D.C.:   GPO, 1978.

This document gives the full text of the hearings before the
Subcommittee on Energy of the Joint Economic Committee concerning
the relationship between energy and employment.   Statements are
made by numerous government officials, corporate officers, special
interest leaders and experts in the field.

12.   Desai, A. V.   "Effects of the Rise in Oil Prices on South Asian
Countries, 1972-78," International Labor Review, Vol. 120, No. 2, March-
April, 1981, pp. 129-147.

The article discusses the effects of increase in oil prices of
1973-74 on four South Asian countries (Bangladesh, India, Pakistan
and Sri Lanka).   The rise in oil prices and the concomitant worsen-
ing of the terms of trade transferred real income abroad from South
Asia.   It also slowed down the build-up of productive capacity.
Employment declined but increased in energy industries industries
competing with oil, namely coal and electricity.   A fall in real
income of one percent would amount to 2 million workers in India
and 200,000 in Bangladesh or Pakistan.   The use in oil prices did
not lead any country to curtail consumption except Sri Lanka.   The
replacement of oil by other fuels proved easier in industry than in
other sectors.   The rise in oil prices made no difference to the
pace of mechanization in agriculture which had already begun.
After 1973, the electrification of pumps was accelerated in relation to intensifying irrigation.   The South Asian economies
appear to have coped with rising oil prices by turning to smaller
vehicles, interfuel substitution, and electrification of pumps.
More options are opened to the economies in the face of more oil
price rises.   This adoption would impact the future growth in South
Asia.

13.   Executive Office of the President.   Energy Policy & Planning.   The
National Energy Plan.   Washington, D.C.:   U.S. Government Printing
Office, April 29, 1977.

The cornerstone of this National Energy Plan is energy conservation.   This plan followed the U.S. energy crisis and naturally
capitalized on the imbalance between the increasing demand for
energy and diminishing supplies of oil and natural gas.   If properly implemented the plan is fully compatible with economic
growth, the development of new industries and the creation of new
jobs.   In fact, in order to effectively prevent an energy crisis,
economic growth with high levels of production and employment
should be maintained.   The salient features of the National Energy
Plan are: 1) conservation and fuel efficiency, 2) rational pricing
and production policies, 3) reasonable certainty and stability in
government policies, 4) substitution of abundant energy resources
for those in short supply, and 5) development of non-conventional

technologies for the future. Finally, the goals of the plan as set forth for 1985 are 1) to reduce the annual growth of total energy demand to below 2 percent, 2) to reduce gasoline consumption 10 percent below its current level, 3) to reduce oil imports from 16 million barrels per day to 6 million or about one-eight of total energy consumption, 4) to establish a strategic Petroleum Reserve of 1 billion barrels, 5) to increase coal consumption by two-thirds, 6) to meet minimum energy efficiency standards in all buildings and residential homes, and 7) to use solar energy in more than 2½ million homes.

The U.S. would gain by adopting the outlined measures to achieve these set goals before world oil production reaches its capacity limitations. Furthermore a macro analysis of the program points at such energy conservation initiatives as contributing to production and employment and avoiding inflation.

14. Fallen-Bailey, Darrel G. And Byer, Trevor A. Energy Options and Policy Issues in Developing Countries. Washington, D.C.: The World Bank, August 1979. Staff Working Paper No. 350.

Energy policy is critical to the national development of the developing countries and to the oil-importing ones in particular. The paper reviews their energy resources and the substitutes for imported oil (coal, and hydropower, and natural gas) including the non-conventional ones. These potential energy resources need to be developed to reduce the dependency on imported energy. It describes the need for implementing national energy planning, energy demand management, conservation and pricing policy. Energy development strategies are examined for three groups of countries: energy surplus, energy balanced, and energy deficient countries. A National energy plan should address three different levels: 1) energy development in relation to the national goals, 2) relationship between different subsectors within the energy sector, and 3) optimal policy or management of each subsector. It is necessary to have detailed information on the structure of total and commercial energy demand and an inventory of national energy resources. A national Energy Accounting System (NEAS) would be useful. Effective energy planning relies on the efforts of high quality specialized personnel. They should coordinate their tasks with other appropriate departments. Broad bilateral or multilateral arrangements can provide the basis for training a cadre of capable managers. In short, effective energy planning requires a data base, resource inventory, the methodology, the skilled manpower and the institutional framework for its implementation. Policy issues associated with fossil fuel development are discussed in relation to the legislative/administrative, financial, technical, and socio-environmental set-ups. The study discusses the options for the development of electric power. Finally, a rational pricing policy is very important for national energy policy.

15. Fayad, Marwan and Motamen, Homa. The Economics of the Petrochemical Industry. New York: St. Martin's Press, 1986.

This book studies the development of the petrochemical industry, its changing structure, its production costs and the role played by the main agents of petrochemical production. The production and consumption patterns of the major petrochemical products have been analyzed for North America, Western Europe and Japan. In particular, the British petrochemical industry is discussed, as well as its status in the developing countries where the production of petrochemicals would continue to grow at relatively high rates throughout this decade. It is maintained that the main determinants for the growth of this sector are the size of the market and industrial output. This is the case of Brazil and South Korea. It is anticipated that the oil-producing developing nations would play a significant role in the production and export of these products by 1990. These countries face the real challenges of developing their managerial and technical skills to reap the benefits of the joint venture arrangements and to reduce their reliance on foreign labor.

16. Federal Energy Administration. National Energy Information Center. Report to Congress on the Economic Impact on Energy Actions, as required by Public Law 93-275, Section 18. Washington, D.C.: U.S. Government Printing Office, May 1976. FEA/B-76/351

The first section of this report describes the economic impact of the energy shortages between April 1, 1976 and June 30, 1977. The severe weather and the shortage of natural gas during this time triggered serious industrial layoffs throughout the Middle Atlantic, Midwest and Southeast regions. At the peak of these adverse conditions, in early February, an estimated 1.2 to 1.5 million persons were affected. "Affected persons" in this study includes not only those that were unemployed but those who were sent home with partial pay or who had their hours reduced. Also over 8,500 reported plant closings were noted. Actual loss of employment as defined by the U.S. Department of Labor was approximately 114,000 during this time.

This report also evaluates the economic effects of actions by the Federal Energy Administration during this period. Of particular interest is the legislative impact on employment in the industrial and trade sectors. This impact is studied on the national, regional, state and local levels.

The Appendix contains "The Inflationary Impact Evaluation of the Proposed Rule-Making for the State Energy Conservation Program," April 1976. This conservation program encourages states to develop and use methods to conserve energy and use energy efficiently. The analysis shows that these programs can be expected to have a deflationary effect on the economy, lowering unemployment approximately one-tenth of one percent over time.

17. Federal Energy Administration. National Energy Information Center. Report to Congress on the Economic Impact of Energy Actions as required by Public Law 93-275, Section 18(d). Washington, D.C.: Federal Energy Administration, June 1977. FEA/B-77/371

The report discusses the energy shortages between April 1, 1976 and June 30, 1977 and their economic impact. The study shows that the curtailment of the U.S. natural gas supply during the 1976 –

77 heating season (November to March) was approximately 1.5 trillion cubic feet. This fact combined with an abnormally cold winter, temporarily idled 1.2 million workers and resulted in 114,000 more unemployed workers. The areas of the United States that were hardest hit included the Middle Atlantic, Midwest and Southeast.

The report also explores the economic impact of FEA actions taken between April 1,1976 and July 1, 1977 in response to the energy shortages. Among the many effects analyzed was the impact on employment by industrial and trade sectors on a national, regional, state and local level.

18. Gehman, John C. and Allen, Edward L. United Kingdom: Estimates of Future Energy/GDP Relationships. Washington D.C.: ORAU, Institute for Energy Analysis, December 1979. ORAU/IEA-79-25(m)

The U.K. economy is expected to grow in real terms, due for the most part to advances in productivity. An increase in the labor force participation rate as a result of more women entering the labor force--to about 65 percent--should just offset a decline in the workweek. The latter is a result of a preferential shift to more leisure time and will reach 33 hours. With productivity increasing, but at a declining rate, real GDP is projected at 50 percent above the 1976 level.

Turning to a sectoral analysis, we expect the number of households to increase by 15 percent as more individuals choose to live alone. The historical shift from goods production to services is expected to continue, but at a slower pace and by the year 2000 we expect service output to reach 55 percent of GDP. In the transport sector, the historical shift toward the passenger car is expected to saturate at about 70 percent of total ton-miles, while the shift toward struck freight is expected to continue and reach 76 percent of total ton-miles. Goods production is expected to stagnate and could fall to 33 percent of GDP by 2000.

Historically, E/GDP has fallen steadily in the United Kingdom due almost exclusively to industrial conservation (investment in new and more efficient plant and equipment). Conservation should spread to all other sectors of the economy as a result of government policy. We expect the E/GDP ratio to fall by another 28 percent by the year 2000. This implies total energy consumption of 8.7 quads. (ORAU)

19. Hannon, Bruce M. "Energy, Growth and Altruism," in J.E. Bailey (editor). Energy Systems: An Analysis for Engineers and Policy Makers. New York: Marcel Dekker, 1978.

The idea of encouraging a form of altruism to emerge in society is explored relative to self-imposed energy conservation. Three dilemmas are discussed to reflect the complexities of human reactions to the energy shortage. The first dilemma examines trading energy for labor. The idea is to develop industries that are less energy-demanding and more labor-intensive. Capital and labor tend to resist a relative increase in the economic value of energy. Reducing energy use is likely to be opposed by the most powerful unions which are unwilling to give up high-paying jobs so that more people might work. The second dilemma tackles the relationship of income and energy and the revision of personal, industrial and governmental patterns of energy use. The third dilemma centers on respending the dollars saved from energy conservation which would lead to the consumption of more energy. If these dilemmas cannot be taken care of, then some form of government intervention is needed. The author suggests an energy tax as a partial solution or an energy-rationing scheme as a complete solution.

20.   Koepp, Stephen. "Cheap Oil!" Time, April 14, 1986, pp. 62-68.

Cheap oil brings good news to the world consumers. The same plunge has negatively affected the oil producing regions. The oil slide is changing the balance of economic power. Bargain oil will bring a go-go era of healthy growth that could be extended to the early 1990's. In the U.S. bankruptcies and layoffs plague the oil business and the related industries. Unemployment in Louisiana has reached 13.2 percent. The oil plunge by putting domestic producers out of business implies heavier dependence on imported oil estimated to jump to 40-45 percent instead of 33 percent. Between 1973 and 1983, the U.S. economy expanded by almost one third while energy consumption slightly fall. A much lower oil bill will improve the U.S. federal budget deficit and trade deficit. Europe is expected to enjoy a real growth of about 3.5 percent this year. Japan, which imports 99.8 percent of the oil consumed, will be able to save some $23 billion this year. In the Middle East, inflation will jump to 40 percent by 1988 and the region economic growth will slow down or even stagnate. The mass exodus of laid off migrant workers from the Persian Gulf could overtax their home countries and possibly stir political instability. The most immediate threat to the U.S. is financial. Bad loans and fear of default (Mexico, Nigeria) triggered the three U.S. agencies that regulate loans to plan for some contingency rescue measures to take over faltering institutions.

21. Kusterer, K.C. Labor Productivity in Heavy Construction: Impact on Synfuels Program Employment. Argonne, Illinios: Argonne National Laboratory, June 1980. ANL/AA-24 (NTIS)

This study focuses on variations in labor productivity in the heavy construction industry. Productivity is one of a number of factors likely to affect the speed and cost of constructing a synthetic fuels plant. The findings of this study are presented with reference to synthetic fuels plants, but they are relevant to other large energy facilities as well. The data were gathered through a detailed literature search and extensive in-depth interviews with consultants in heavy industrial construction, union officials, and management. In this manner the most important determinants of labor productivity were identified and ranked in terms of relative significance. The type of project under construction is the most important factor affecting the productivity of heavy construction labor. Projects characterized by the the utility work syndrome are large, complex, relatively unique, highly regulated, and have cost-plus contracts and tight deadlines. Such projects generally have lower-than-average levels of labor productivity. Labor productivity is also lowered by worker and management morale problems, due to delays and design changes, and by high levels of unemployment among construction workers. Finally, boomtown condition, caused by workers moving to live near large projects located in rural areas, also are likely to result in below-average labor identified characteristics. Consequently, the findings suggest that labor productivity may well be a problem for the timely development of an economically competitive synthetic fuels industry. (NTIS)

22. Martin, Ricardo and Selowsky, Marcelo. Energy Prices, Substitution and Optimal Borrowing in the Short-Run. An Analysis of Adjustment in Oil-Importing Developing Countries. Washington, D.C.: The World Bank, 1981. Staff Working Paper No. 466.

The response of oil importing developing countries to the 1973-1974 and 1979-1980 oil price shocks was to strongly increase their external borrowing, particularly from private sources. Such borrowing increased from 1.7 percent of their GDP in 1970-1973 to 5.1 percent in 1975. It then increased again from 2.3 percent in 1976-1978 to 3.9 percent in 1980. This heavy extra borrowing from private sources has become a source of concern because it will imply a historical peak of debt service ratios for middle income countries of 29 percent by 1985 (World Development Report, 1980). The Bank and IMF have reacted by opening new lending facilities to respond to these oil induced demands for borrowing, structural adjustment lending in the case of the Bank.

This paper builds a normative framework to evaluate three questions:

- To what extent the increases in indebtedness of developing countries was "excessive" or simply the result of a perfectly rational strategy?

- What borrowing strategies can be expected in the future as the developing countries revise their expectations about the length of time between shocks? (i.e., was the 1973-1974 shock perceived as a one time phenomenon?)

- What is the derived demand (or oil price induced borrowing) to be faced by multilateral institutions providing some amount of concessionary credit, i.e., the interest elasticity of that demand.

The framework used here consists of a short-term model (no factor mobility except for intermediate inputs) of two sectors (traded and nontraded goods). Prices are flexible, and the exchange rate is allowed to float. An optimal borrowing rule is derived by maximizing a welfare function over the planning period. That period, defined by the expected number of years of oil price stability after the shock, is short. (WB)

23. Melvin, J.R. The Effects of Energy Price Changes on Commodity Prices, Interprovincial Trade, and Employment. Toronto: University of Toronto Press, 1976.

The study investigates the effects of petroleum and natural gas price increases on commodity prices and estimates their impact on trade and employment in Ontario, Canada. Assuming a 100 percent increase in energy prices, it was found, based on the Ontario input-output table that the overall commodity price increases would be small. They would be even less in basic manufacturing. Based on Cobb-Douglas utility functions, the Ontario labor force would experience a drop of 2-4 percent in employment. A reduction in the trade balance was found to vary ranging from $65.3 million to $1093.1 million. It is recommended to maintain a policy of price uniformity across the country. The evaluation of different alternative economic policies to offset an increase in prices of petroleum and natural gas have proven to be expensive (subsidies) or inefficient (change in corporate income tax).

24. National Petroleum Council. Committee on Emergency Preparedness. Availability of Materials, Manpower, and Equipment for the Exploration, Drilling, and Production of Oil - 1974-1976. Washington, D.C.: National Petroleum Council, September, 1974.

The purpose of the study is to investigate the availability of materials, manpower, and equipment for the exploration, drilling and production of oil in order to reduce dependence on imports.

The depressed economic environment of oil and gas industry led to decline in the footage drilled (24%) and number of available rigs (20%). The efficiency of drilling rigs has been reduced by delays in the availability of tubular goods and manpower problems. The long-range outlook for drilling activity requires the rapid expansion of drilling equipment manufacturing capacity. Although basic steel output required for drilling is in short supply, it is not expected to present a critical constraint to the drilling activity. The same holds true for manpower. However, it is very important that the industry attracts qualified manpower and that it extends its training programs. Several recommendations were made based on the above assessment. It is important to formulate national energy policies to increase the domestic energy supplies. The prices of oil and gas should be determined by the market forces. In support of drilling expansion, steelmaking capacity should be enhanced as well as the availability of drilling and producing equipment. Finally, economic incentives should be provided for more oil production from the known reservoirs.

25. Organization of Arab Petroleum Exporting Countries. "The Need for Long-Term Joint Arab Strategy on Oil and Development," (Editorial), OAPEC Bulletin, Vol. 12, No. 4, April 1986, p.1.

The Arab economies have been major victims of recent erratic changes in the world oil market. The fluctuations in world oil demand and supply have a magnified impact on Arab revenues, and their repercussions are transmitted to all the economies in the Arab region. The experiences of the past few years clearly demonstrate the pitfalls inherent in the unpredictable character of the oil market, whose adverse consequences are felt in both the upward and downward phases of the cycle. Thus the revenues of the Arab countries jumped from $77 billion in 1978 to $213 billion in 1980, with the expectation that they might rise even higher in future. However, they declined equally suddenly to $114 billion in 1983, and they have been falling ever since, with the prospect of larger reductions due to downward pressures on price and to the depreciation of the dollar.

Such fluctuations would undoubtedly put enormous stresses on the economy of any country. But the fluctuations particularly affect the Arab countries, as their economies are all still in the early stages of development and largely dependent on this commodity with its erratic behavior. The problems have been compounded by the lack of a coordinated long-term Arab strategy on oil and economic development. Instead, Arab policies have been preoccupied with the short-term vagaries of the market, reacting to events over which they exercise little control.

The continuation of such measures will have a damaging impact on the long-term prospects of all the Arab countries. Therefore, far-sighted policies are needed to counteract the adverse consequences of these measures and to reduce the effect of overdependence on oil. Any measures adopted to deal with short-term problems should also consider their implications on the Arab economies in the decades to come. Needless to say, the approach should be based on the coordination of development plans and on cooperation between the Arab countries to minimize the impact of short-term turbulence. The political differences that appear sometimes between Arab regimes should be dealt with as temporary phenomena and should not be allowed to impinge on the realization of their strategy objectives. Intra-Arab organizations and joint institutions, if given more support and confidence from member states, can make this very difficult task possible. (OAPEC)

26. Quammen, David. Appropriate Jobs: Common Goals of Labor and Appropriate Technology. Butte, Montana: National Center for Appropriate Technology, 1980.

Appropriate technology (AT) (also referred to as alternative technology or the soft path) is custom-fit to people and their communities. The publication addresses different issues. First, it examines the flaws in the argument linking energy use with employment. Both correlate to some other factors that have increased over time (e.g. total output and total population). It distinguishes between decrease in energy demand with sudden disruptions of energy supply. While conservation results in reduced energy use, its impact will be higher employment. Five factors are listed to affect energy use level: population growth, energy price, personal income, technological efficiency and the capital stock. Second, the energy supply and the energy-intensive industries employ only 10 percent of the total workforce. Third, these industries use up a very high proportion of capital. The average investment required to create one job in manufacturing is $19,500 compared to $41,000 in energy-intensive industries. This figure is much higher for the energy-supply industry ranging from $115,000 to $300,000. Fourth, overemphasis on the production of electricity to waste on inappropriate uses deprives the workers from potential jobs. One dollar spent by a consumer on electricity produces less employment than a dollar spent on any other purchase (e.g. durables, food and clothing). Fifth, conservation by applying technical adjustments to leaks in industrial, commercial and domestic use can lead to additional energy supply. Conservation is labor-intensive. It can create more jobs than development of new supplies. The adoption of conservation and solar option technologies could create three times as many jobs as the nuclear option and would provide double the energy. Sixth, the solar option has many supporters, among whom are several unions (e.g. Sheet Metal Workers International). Solar technology yields four times as many jobs per million dollars invested relative to nuclear generation. But government and industry have not been ardent supporters. Seventh, the various energy-supply options offered by appropriate technology offer healthy and stable workplaces for the workers.

27. Starr, Chauncey and Stanford, Field. "Economic Growth, Employment and Energy," Energy Policy, Vol. 7, December 1979, pp. 321-328.

The article comprehensively describes the interaction between economic growth, employment and energy use. A model of the energy-productivity system is used to estimate the amount of energy that the U.S. will need to achieve social progress in the year 2000.

In the past, increased labor productivity has more than offset the decline in the annual hours worked. Assuming that this is a continuous trend, an estimate of the employment level should provide an estimate of the total primary energy associated with that level. An equation is given based on this assumption. The equation forecasts that an employment level in the year 2000 will exist that will require an energy input of 170×10^5 Btus. The authors suggest, with this trend in mind, that the U.S. adopt a primary energy supply target for the year 2000 of 150×10^{15} Btus per year. This is necessary because of the direct relationship between the demand for primary energy and the level of employment, the time worked, and the average output per employee.

28. Third Arab Energy Conference. "Country Paper-State of Kuwait." Paper presented at the Third Arab Energy Conference - Energy and Cooperation, May 4- 9, 1985, Algiers, Algeria. Safat, Kuwait: OAPEC, 1985.

This paper describes the current economic condition as it relates to energy in the State of Kuwait. The paper discusses consumption patterns, energy sources, prices in local market, petroleum industries and manpower requirements, institutional set-up, joint Arab ventures as well as the regional and international participation. In relation to manpower in the energy field the number of employed persons increased from 16,530 to 27,290 between mid-1971 and 1983. A large part of this increase was attributed to petroleum-related activities. Power-stations, when compared with the growth in electricity production, experienced only a modest increase. (OAPEC)

29. U. S. Congress. Senate. Committee on Labor and Public Welfare. Subcommittee on Employment, Poverty and Migratory Labor. Unemployment and the Energy Crisis, 1974. Los Angeles, California, February 14, 1974. Washington, D.C.: GPO, 1974.

The hearings assess the current unemployment situation as affected by the energy crisis of 1974, with special reference to the State of California. Witnesses are drawn from government, business, labor organizations, and academia. These issues addressed cover the industries and occupations hit the hardest (the cases of the aerospace and plastic industries are presented), the role of CETA manpower training, and public service employment the unemployment insurance program as well as the impact on women workers is also investigated.

30. U.S. Department of Labor. Secretary of Labor's Report on the Impact of Energy Shortages on Manpower Needs. Washington, D.C.: U.S. Department of Labor, March 1974.

The study examines the current and prospective impacts of energy shortages on employment and unemployment. It also reviews the actions undertaken by the Department of Labor (DOL) to alleviate such employment impact. The analysis focuses on the primary effects of energy shortage, i.e. the secondary effects are not considered. The first part of the study reviews the impact on current employment in terms of unemployment rate, geographic areas, industries and occupations affected. As to future employment, it is believed that the search for alternative energy sources and more intensive utilization of domestically available fuels should promote the generation of many new jobs in several industries. The search for new energy sources will have major manpower implications for the extractive industries (coal mining, crude petroleum and natural gas extraction), petroleum refining and electric utilities. Employment is estimated to increase by 81 percent covering a wide variety of occupations from unskilled to high level manpower. DOL has adopted several programs to address the problems of employment associated with energy shortage. Current initiatives include increase staffing of unemployment compensation, more efficient counseling and placement of displaced workers, manpower training and public service employment under CETA (Comprehensive Employment and Training Act), augmented data search to figure out the employment effects of energy crisis, and use of interindustry information and its manpower effects. A series of additional measures were recommended to Congress for action (e.g., extension of unemployment benefits, additional appropriations under CETA).

31. The World Bank. The Energy Transition in Developing Countries. Washington, D.C.: The World Bank, 1983.

The rise in the price of energy during the seventies has greatly affected the growth prospects of the developing countries. They need to actively undertake programs of energy conservation and substitution. To reduce foreign oil dependence, they need to design and implement more appropriate energy strategies. This effort requires better management both within enterprises supplying energy and at the national level in order to identify and invest in domestic energy resources. It is maintained that the quality of management is the key to future investments. The planning and management of energy investments are complex due to uncertainty and risk, new technology, lumpiness of investment, and limited private sector involvement. Linkages are important in investment programming and in decisions affecting the structure of prices. Weaknesses in management include personnel insufficient training and experience, inadequate facilities and ill-designed curricula as well as poor management practices. These are complicated by low levels of education skills of the workforce of the energy sector and the unavailability of specialized consultants. Energy supply activities are undertaken by government or public enterprises. Bureaucratic delays, regulated wage and salary structures have more negative manpower implications. These problems are quite acute in the power and coal subsectors. The main effort to improve energy management has to originate in the countries themselves. Recommended actions include: upgrading the skills of staff and coordination of enterprise plans by planning team. Yet, there is great scope for external assistance in improving enterprise management structures, especially in relation to training. A national energy management program should focus on four measures: 1) energy pricing policies, 2) taxation and fiscal incentives, 3) direct capital allocation, and 4) technical assistance. The report also reviews the energy supply prospects and the associated financial resource requirements.

2
Energy Labor Demand

32. Ahuja, Y. L. "Manpower and Training Implications for Energy
Development in India," Energy Management, January-March, 1982, pp.
15-18.

This paper examines the manpower and training implications of the
development of non-renewable sources of energy in India. It
reviews the sources of energy in terms of power, petroleum and
solar energy. For power generation, manpower requirement needs are
estimated to be 32,000 persons of various levels between 1978-83.
For transmission, distribution and rural electrification, about
30,000 to 40,000 might be required. The present training facilities are not adequate to cope with these new demands and need to be
enlarged. For petroleum, the annual employment growth rate is low
(1%). An anticipated addition in refinery capacity would require
about 2600 more persons and another 6000 persons are needed for the
expansion of exploration and production. To meet energy demand,
India has to turn to solar energy. To develop this source requires
qualified manpower. It is recommended to adopt a multicraft
approach to training to provide flexibility to meet such training
needs.

33. Al-Kamer, Jaseem. "Future Demand Expectations of Energy in
Kuwait," Proceedings of Second Arab Energy Conference in Doha, Qatar -
March 1982 - Part Four. Kuwait: OAPEC, 1982 pp. 221-237. (in Arabic)

The recent economic and social developments in Kuwait have led to
an ever increasing level of energy consumption. The main purpose
of this paper is to examine the patterns of total energy consumption in Kuwait. It specifically outlines the factors that affect
present and future energy consumption (e.g., population growth,
price and income trends). Population growth and higher standards
of living have definitely resulted in increasing the consumption of
electricity and petroleum products in Kuwait.

34. American Nuclear Society. Scientific and Technical Manpower
Requirements of Selected Sectors of the Atomic Energy Field. ANS
Nuclear Manpower Survey, Final Report. Hinsdale, Illinois: ANS,
August. 19, 1970. 5210-0267 (GPO)

The study presents data on the technical manpower requirements of selected sectors (private industry, electric utilities and the educational institutions) of the atomic energy field between July 1964 and December 1973. They cover only those who spend or will spend 50 percent of their working time in atomic energy activities. The study focuses on the need for nuclear degreed scientists and engineers. Also, the study examines the relevance of the type of education received to the needs of the industry. The general findings reveal that demand slightly outweighs supply for nuclear scientists and engineers with MS's and BS's. However, there is a greater projected supply of nuclear scientists and engineers with PhDs than the estimated needed demand. This is understandable given that private industry and the electric utilities are switching to product development and operation. The organizations expect to face a critical shortage in the fields of mechanical and electric/electronic engineering. A larger number of technicians would be hired to relieve the engineers of some of their functions. The demand, therefore, for technicians would outstrip the available supply. The presentation of statistical data is given separately for the private industry sector of the atomic energy field (e.g., uranium milling, reactors, radioactive waste disposal), electric power utilities and educational institutions.

35. Andrews, John. "Jobs Energy and Economic Growth in Australia" in Mark Diesendorf (editor). Energy and People. Forest Grove, Oregon: International Scholarly Book Service, 1980.

Australia compares very poorly with other developed countries in the amount of research done to investigate alternative energy strategies and their socioeconomic and political ramifications. An important contribution would be to analyze the different employment impacts of the alternative energy paths. Two questions are raised:

1)   Does the use of more energy lead to more jobs? It is argued that this is a myth. Economic growth calls for the use of more energy. It appeared as if energy expansion has caused an increase in jobs. Rather, it is expanding demand that has led to expanding production and employment.

2)   Can zero energy growth support full employment? Employment opportunities in a low or zero energy growth future for Australia are likely to be far better than in the high energy growth future currently planned. Long term slowing of energy growth signalled by appropriate public policies and slowly rising energy prices would actually increase employment. The emphasis, here, is on the job creating potential of energy conservation. But, economic and political changes, in addition to energy changes, are warranted.

36. Arab Labor Organization and Arab Petroleum Training Institute. "Human Resources and Manpower, Research and Training for Future Energy Needs in the Arab World," Proceedings of Second Arab Energy Conference in Doha, Qatar - March 1982. Kuwait: OAPEC, 1982, pp. 97-134. (in Arabic)

The paper deals with the nature and scope of Arab human resources and the manpower needed for energy during the next twenty years. It addressed the main features of manpower in the Arab World:

growth rates, limited participation of women, low productivity, unbalanced manpower distribution among the various economic sectors and the inadequacy of training and educational systems. The problems of the Arab brain drain and the migration of Arab manpower to developed countries as well as those of imported labor into the Arab world, specifically from Southeast Asia were discussed. Based on increased development needs, a manpower deficit is foreseen by 1985. The paper, in particular, concentrates on the petroleum industry due to the major role it plays in the economies of most Arab countries. Its characteristics and those of its labor force are outlined stressing the difficulties of meeting its future manpower needs.

37. Baker, Joe G. and Olsen, Kathryn. Occupational Employment in Nuclear or Nuclear - Related Activities, 1981. Washington, D.C.: U.S. Department of Energy, April 1982. ORAU--197, DE82 014451

This report describes 1981 employment in nuclear-related activities and compares it to previous years. Employment characteristics examined include detailed occupations of scientists, engineers, and technicians; worker involvement in research and development activities; employment by industrial segment (e.g., reactor operation and maintenance, weapons production, and commercial laboratory services); employment by establishment type (government-owned, contractor-operated [GOCO], private, and nonprofit); regional employment; and employment by establishment size.

Total 1981 nuclear-related employment is estimated to be 249,500--a growth of 22,600 workers over the 1977 total. GOCO workers make up 36.9 percent of this total. Among all the nuclear-related workers, scientists comprise 5.1 percent; engineers, 15.3 percent; and technicians, 17.5 percent; the remaining 62.1 percent is composed of managers, skilled craft and clerical workers, and other support services. Research and development involvement has declined from the 1977 survey results, with 60 percent of scientists and 27.0 percent of engineers currently involved in R&D. The largest single industrial segment activity is weapons development (16.9 percent of total employment), followed closely by reactor operation and maintenance employment (16.7 percent). There has been considerable change in the distribution of employment by industrial segment from 1977 to 1981; the reactor and reactor component design and manufacturing segment fell by over 9,700 workers while reactor operator and maintenance employment grew by over 24,000 workers. (ORAU)

38. Baker, Joe Garrett. "Labor Allocation and Western Energy Development." PhD Dissertation, University of Utah. March 1977.

The achievement of energy independence would have a major impact on future manpower requirements. The manpower impact of energy development will be concentrated as a consequence of the spatial distribution of the industry. The objective of this research effort is to examine the mechanisms of labor allocation in the small, rural energy impacted communities of Rocky Mountain Northern Great Plains region. For this purpose, three case studies were undertaken. Most of the energy development in the region centers around coal fired electricity production (underground, surface

mining and power plant construction and operation. A conceptual
model of information/allocation is discussed. Empirical evidence
has shown that the high wage vacancies in the energy related
occupations resulted in considerable labor mobility and supply
response. Migration played a major role in the overall labor
supply response. Rural workers were willing to commute considerable distances for employment. The information/allocation system
fits the internal labor market system. A "two-phase" system is in
operation. The initial quantitative needs for the operational
workforce are satisfied by high wage vacancies and labor mobility.
The qualitative dimensions are met by individual firm pricing,
allocation and skill acquisition mechanisms. The findings indicate
that the information/allocation mechanisms are quite adequate. One
major constraints to both phases of the allocation mechanism was
the "quality of life" aspects of the communities. Such problems
led to high rates of labor turnover. The study recommends some
policy options to improve the manpower aspects of energy development.

39. Baron, Thomas. "Consequences of Divestiture for R & D and the
Development of Alternate Energy Sources," in David J. Teece (editor). R
& D in Energy. Stanford, California: Institute for Energy Studies,
August 1977, pp. 147-174.

Forced divestiture, vertical or horizontal, will negatively impact
R & D and the transfer of technology to new processes and products.
It would limit the free flow of technical information among different disciplines which are interrelated in an integrated company.
The overlap of technologies in various parts of the oil industry
will not be modified by the creation of artificial and abrupt legal
boundaries by divestiture. There is an important advantage in the
common use of experts in different fields as manifested by central
R & D groups, which integrated oil companies use but which fragmented companies do not use. The multidisciplinary nature of the
integrated oil companies is most appropriate for the effective
technology transfer necessary for the development of alternate
fuels. With divestiture, the participants would require substantial education to bring them up to the technological levels in all
fields which now prevail in the oil industries. The management of
the new participants would be more difficult in relation to the
selection between competing projects and alternatives as well as
the raising of the necessary capital.

40. Baroudi, Nouhad. "Energy Supply and Demand Balances in the Arab
World, 1985 - 2000," Proceedings of Second Energy Conference - Doha,
Qatar, March 1982. Kuwait: OAPEC, 1982. (in Arabic)

The energy status of the Arab World is examined in terms of sources
and availability in order to project the supply and demand for
energy over the period 1985-2000. Projected energy balances are
developed for each type of fuel showing primary energy production,
exports, imports, energy conversion and final consumption. Such
projections are carried out within the framework of a regional
energy balance model. According to the study, energy demand in
Arab countries would reach 667 Mtoe by year 2000 compared to 248
Mtoe in 1985. Total energy production was forecast to use to 1,987

Mtoe by the end of the century reaching 1,434 Mtoe by 1985. Crude oil output would account for 1,173 Mtoe of total energy production in 1985 increasing to 1,431 Mtoe in 2000. A clearly spelled- out Arab oil production strategy would constitute an important factor to assess future world oil supply availabilities. The study attempts to integrate the Arab world projections in a purely illustrative picture of future world primary energy and oil supply and demand.

41. Batelle Columbus Laboratories. Solar Energy Employment and Requirements 1978-1983. Washington, D.C.: U.S. Department of Energy, 1980; reprint ed., San Meteo, California: Solar Energy Information Services (SEIS), 1981.

This study provides the number, occupational distribution and characteristics of people and establishments that were engaged in solar energy work in 1978. It also projects solar manpower require-ments through 1983. The scope of the study focuses on profes-sional, technical and skilled craft occupations in all types of solar energy technologies and applications. The analysis provides a description of the status of manpower in the solar energy area and develops and applies a methodology for projecting manpower requirements in solar energy.

The results estimated that approximately 22,500 employees were engaged in solar energy work in 1978. However, not all employees were full-time with the average hours spent on solar-related work being around 30 hours a week. Projections for 1981 showed that full-time commercial solar employment will increase 137 percent in 1981 and 203 percent in 1983. Full-time equivalent employment is expected to double by 1981 and increase by 170 percent by 1983.

Five recommendations are presented to the Department of Energy based on this study:

1. To carry periodic surveys of establishments engaged in solar energy activities to determine employment and occupational distributions.

2. To identify solar energy employed in existing occupational surveys (e.g. National Sample of Scientists and Engineers National Industry Occupation Employment Sample).

3. To obtain information concerning solar energy manpower supply.

4. To obtain improved estimates of labor requirements for produc-tion and installation of different types of solar energy systems.

5. To obtain improved regional and state projections of future solar energy manpower and occupational needs.

42. Blair, L.M. "Occupational Employment Trends in Selected Nuclear Industry Segments in the United States of America." Paper presented at the International Atomic Energy Agency Symposium - Manpower Requirements and Development for Nuclear Programmes, Saclay, 2-6, April, 1979. Vienna: IAEA, 1980. IAEA-SM-238/21

The United States of America's nuclear energy industry expanded between 1968 and 1977, with total employment increasing by approximately 60 percent. Between 1973 and 1977 employment grew at a rate of 6.8% per year. The nuclear industry appears to have reached a mature status with the primary focus on commercial activities. The relative number of workers involved in research and development activities, outside of contract research facilities, has declined considerably since 1968 but appears to have stabilized. The industry labour force still has a relatively high proportion (43%) of scientific, engineering and technical workers. The occupational employment composition appears to have stabilized in the various nuclear segments indicating the emergence of longer run occupational distribution patterns. Employment expanded rapidly between 1968 and 1977 in most nuclear segments, with the exception of the research and development segment, where employment decreased by one-third. The present uncertainties concerning nuclear power development could have substantial impacts on the nuclear-related scientific, engineering, and technical labour force if a sizeable contraction occurs in reactor design of nuclear facilities. (IAEA)

43. Blair, Larry M. and Barker, Larry. An Analysis of Nuclear Related Technician Manpower in the Western States. Washington, D.C.: Energy Research and Development Administration, November 1975. ERDA-78 UC-2 (NTIS)

This survey covers the twelve states served by the Western Interstate Nuclear Board (WINB). It provides a good data base on the employment and training of nuclear related technicians in the western states. The survey has accounted for approximately 95 percent of the total nuclear related technician employment in the states under study. In January 1975, about 17,000 nuclear related technicians were employed in the western states with an annual growth rate of 10 percent projected for the immediate future. The largest single employer group is U.S. ERDA contractors. It is projected, however, that private organizations and utilities would take the lead. The technician subgroups include: 1) nuclear research, production and reactor operation, 2) test and measurement, 3) instrumentation techniques, 4) nuclear medical and health, 5) other. A twenty percent annual increase in additional demand is projected for the period 1975-77. Shortages are reported for the first and second subgroup and a surplus appears for the fourth subgroup. The state distribution indicates that California alone accounts for nearly 45 percent of the total employment of nuclear related technicians.

44. Brock, H. W.; Murray, G. R.; McConnell, J. D.; and Snipes, J.C. Strategic Implications of Solar Energy For Employment of Sheet Metal Workers. Menlo Park, California: Stanford Research Institute, June 1975.

The Stanford Research Institute (SRI) analyzed the implications of solar energy on employment for Sheet Metal Workers International Association (SMWIA). For the solar heating/cooling industry, a $2 billion market is predicted. The study reports about $250 to 300 million would go to wages for sheet metal workers. Government research expenditures were devoted to solar energy. What are the likely impacts of the heating, ventilating, and air conditioning (HVAC) industry and sheet metal employment? The study assesses the future outlook for energy in the United States and the future of solar energy, in particular and the related technological develop-ments. It evaluates the impacts of solar energy on sheet metal work and offers recommendations to the union, accordingly.

The findings reported point out that solar heating and cooling will represent a small percentage of energy from all sources this century. Its share (5 percent) of total research and development finding for fiscal 1975 was the lowest relative to other energy areas (e.g. nuclear, coal). As solar and cooling systems will be installed in parallel with conventional systems (rather than in lieu of), sheet metal employment opportunities will be increased, not decreased, by the development of such systems. It is expected that the training skills for solar heating and cooling will be given to those who handle the installations. Sheet metal work for the construction industry is estimated to grow by one-third over the next decade. The sheet metal industry and its Union will not be affected by the introduction of solar heating and cooling systems. Instead, the Union should turn its attention to other opportunities (e.g. residential construction).

45. Brookes, L. G. "Nuclear Energy = More Jobs?"   Energy Manager, July/ August, 1979, pp. 21-23.

This article focuses on the energy/jobs debate. Does nuclear energy represent a poor bargain in terms of money invested per job created? This argument is challenged from a pro-nuclear stand. The issue of capital-intensive versus labor-intensive systems is discussed. Capital-intensive systems produce more output and income per worker. The adoption of such technology has contributed to the progress and affluence of the industrial nations of the world. Capital accumulation has, in essence, alleviated the constraints on population, employment and incomes. In order to produce higher total employment, capital per worker must steadily increase. Capital-intensive energy does not lead to unemployment. The reverse is true. The fallacy of composition is invoked to discard the belief that labor-intensive technology creates more employment than modern technology.

46. Brown, Robert J. "Energy-Employment: The Critical Dependency in the U.S. Economy." Paper presented at the National Commission for Manpower Policy, San Francisco, October 14, 1976.

This paper emphasizes the urgency to develop a contingency planning framework for the U.S. to handle any other major energy inter-ruption. It is recommended that the Department of Labor assumes this responsibility. The premise is that the U.S. is vulnerable to a major and prolonged energy cutback. The employment dislocations of the 1973 oil embargo were significant. Another interruption would, therefore, have another major employment impact. The private sector firms have an important responsibility to insure adequate sources of trained manpower. The firms need to supply accurate and timely information on their development plans. Companies in the energy industries have cooperated with organized labor which has proven to be very useful. Organized labor occupies a pivotal position in the labor supply solution. The report discusses the employment implications of expanded energy production over the next decade. At the regional level, (Federal Regions VIII) energy shortage is analyzed in terms of the geographic dispersion of employment dislocation and the socioeconomic impact of rapid energy development. Policy makers must give adequate attention to the non-market conditions as well as to the training, retraining and mobility aspects of the labor market.

47.   Buchsbaum, Steven. Jobs and Energy: The Employment and Economic Impacts of Nuclear Power, Conservation and Other Energy Options. New York: Council of Economic Priorities, 1979.

This study compares employment (number and types of jobs) to be created by energy conservation and solar energy with that provided by conventional fuels and by building/operating new nuclear plants. The Council of Economic Priorities (CEP) has focused on one region as a pilot (Nassau and Suffolk counties on eastern Long Island in New York). The energy and employment aspects of Long Island are typical of other regions. Hence, the findings could be easily generalized. Different scenarios (energy conservation and solar energy use) provide for the net creation of an average of 10,000 to 13,000 jobs during the next four decades. The regional impact in the counties under study reflects the reduction of unemployment from 6.3 percent in 1979 to 5.5 percent.

48.   Chewning, J. S. "Scientists, Engineers and Technicians in Nuclear Reactor Operation and Maintenance." Paper presented at the International Atomic Energy Agency Symposium - "Manpower Requirements and Development for Nuclear Programmes, Saclay, 2-6 April, 1979. Vienna: IAEA, 1980. IAEA-SM-28/18

Between 1962 and 1977 the number of nuclear reactors in the United States of America increased from 4 to 65, and the total capacity increased from 730 to 47013 MW. Employment in the reactor operation and maintenance sector, which increased correspondingly from 633 to 17,270, showed the earmarks of a maturing industry. By the end of that 15-year span, fewer workers were involved in research and development activities, and the proportion of scientists and engineers had decreased as the duties and responsibilities became more standardized and routine and could be taken over by highly trained technicians. There were also subtle changes in the discipline mixes. Nuclear and reactor engineers took their place in the labour force in increasing numbers as nuclear engineering was recognized as a distinct occupation, and there was a corresponding decrease in the proportion of more traditional engineering disciplines. Life science disciplines increased as concern grew for the health and safety of nuclear workers and the general public, and the physical science disciplines decreased in importance as proportionally less research and development was carried out in reactor operation and maintenance. A profile of nuclear power plant personnel drawn from refined data shows that the industry has truly 'come of age.' By far the largest group of workers is made up of technicians, with the second largest group made up of skilled

craftworkers.   Less than 30% of all workers in nuclear power
operation and maintenance in 1977 were in professional occupations.
(IAEA)

49. Cogan, John; Johnson, Bruce M.; and Ward, Michael P.   Energy and
Jobs: A Long Run Analysis.   Los Angeles: Institute for Economic
Research, UCLA, July 1976.

The focus of the analysis is on the long-run implications of
alternative energy policies in terms of 1) aggregate U.S. employment, 2) real gross national product, 3) subsidization of crude
petroleum products, 4) taxation of petroleum consumption, and 5)
subsidization of coal production.   The Hudson—Jergenson econometric
model is used to simulate those policies for 1980 and 1985.   The
empirical findings indicate: 1)   Energy policies geared to reduce
import dependence through higher energy prices raise the demand for
labor.   2)   Import reducing policies (except for decontrol and a
tax on crude oil) tend to reduce real GNP per capita.   3)   Coal
production subsidies have an insignificant impact on reducing oil
imports or stimulating output and employment.   4)   Decontrol of
domestic crude oil and natural gas industries represents the
least-cost strategy for reducing energy imports.

50. Construction Analysis Services.   Forecasts of On-Site and Off-Site
Occupational Requirements for Energy Development in the United States,
1982-2000.   Knoxville, Tennessee: The University of Tennessee, November
1982.

This analysis forecasts labor requirements in the U.S. to build,
operate and maintain new capacity in the energy sector through the
year 2000.   The report finds that approximately 87,000 new on-site
jobs per year will be created to operate and maintain the new
facilities.   Also, approximately 531,000 jobs will be created for
construction.   Additionally, 320,000 support positions will be
needed annually.

In 1990, the largest demand for construction will occur: 660,000
jobs will be generated.   Operation and maintenance jobs grow at a
constant rate of 87,000 throughout the period.   The labor requirements for operation and maintenance will be made up of 26 percent
engineers, 23 percent non-technical workers, and 51 percent craft
workers.   Construction labor requirements will be 15 percent
engineers, 3 percent non-technical workers and 82 percent craft
workers.   Large job increases can be expected among operating
engineers, laborers, mechanics, electricians and pipefitters in the
craft category and supervisors/managers, technicians, and plant
operators in the technical category.

The report also describes the different labor requirements for ten
major regions in the United States.   It is indicated that the
requirements vary widely from region to region.   The significant
increases in energy-related job growth for the nation and the ten
Federal regions discussed could result in potential supply-demand
imbalances for some occupations.   The appendix presents the methods
of forecasting labor requirements for the construction, operation
and maintenance of energy projects.

51. Cortes, Mariluz and Bocock, Peter. North-South Technology Transfer- A Case Study of Petrochemicals in Latin America. Washington, D.C.: International Bank for Reconstruction and Development - The World Bank, 1984.

The study examines the transfer of petrochemical technology to Latin America's industrializing economies. The study covers 280 petrochemical plants in seven specific countries: Argentina, Brazil, Chile, Colombia, Mexico, Peru and Venezuela. The focus is on the transfer process in terms of what is transferred, who is involved, and under what terms and conditions transfers take place. There is a strong evidence for a marked bifurcation of ownership of processes by type of owner and product group, with producers owning all processes for the manufacture of final products and non-producers predominating in the ownership of processes for making basic products. Country and market factors might affect the particular type of contractual arrangement used for transfers of technology. The main determinants of the type of contractual arrangements used in petrochemical technology transfer are, in order of importance, type of product, recipient's country, and suppliers' country. More recently the terms of the contract were liberalized as non-producer suppliers have increased their share of transfers and as producers developed flexible responses to recipient's legislation limiting foreign participation.

52. Critchlow, Robert V. "Technology and Labor in Electric Power and Gas Industry," Monthly Labor Review, November 1978, pp. 18-22.

Technology is affecting the occupational structure of the electric power and gas industry. The growth of nuclear power plants requires a more highly skilled work force. More frequent use of computers requires higher employment in scientific, technical and managerial occupations. Generally, nuclear plants have larger and more highly trained work forces than do fossil-fuel plants. There may be a long-term decline occurring in the rate of productivity growth. Labor requirements per unit of output may not continue to decline as much as they did over the past 10 to 15 years. This is because the size of the generating plant is not expected to increase as it did in the past. Also the labor requirements of nuclear powered and coal fired plants are relatively high and these are expected to be the primary source of electric power in the future. Finally, the utility industry has developed training programs to introduce its employees to new technologies.

53. Csik, B.J. "Manpower Requirements for Nuclear Power in Developing Countries." Paper presented at the International Atomic Energy Symposium - Manpower Requirements and Development for Nuclear Programmes, Saclay, 2-6 April, 1979. Vienna: IAEA, 1980. IAEA-SM-238/42

It is recognized that each country has its individual unique characteristics and that there is no typical or average developing country. Common conditions represent exceptions, rather than the rule. Manpower requirements, however, are created by the tasks to be performed and activities to be carried out at each definite stage of a nuclear power project or programme. These tasks and activities, as well as the manpower requirements they create, are of a similar nature for any country, subject to the influence of prevailing local conditions. First, successive stages of the evolution of a nuclear power programme are defined. These are: pre-planning, planning, study and procurement, construction, operation of the first plant, confirmed and self-sufficient in implementing nuclear power projects. The developing countries are then classified according to the present stage of their evolution. Finally, the present and future manpower requirements of each country or group of countries are estimated. No attempt has been made to try to establish any precise data for any country in particular. The results obtained are global estimates, intended as indications of trends and of orders of magnitude. It is found that the developing world's present manpower requirements for nuclear power are of the order of 100,000 people, of which about 20,000 need specialized nuclear training. By the year 2000, for an installed nuclear capacity of 150 to 200 GW, overall manpower requirements should increase to more than 500, 000 which would include 130, 000 with specialized nuclear training. (IAEA)

54. Daneker, Gail and Grossman, Richard. Energy, Jobs and the Economy. Boston, Massachusetts: Alyson Publications, 1979.

This book dispels the myth that production and consumption of traditional energy sources expand the job market. It contends that corporations use energy to promote automation and the workers initially hired to build and start the plant eventually are no longer needed. They are replaced by the machines that they build.

Some solutions are offered in order to break the cycle and guarantee jobs. The first is conservation. Fifty percent of energy used by American industry is wasted. The cheapest way to acquire more energy is to close the gaps and clean the waste using human labor. A second solution is to turn to the sun as a source of energy. The industry is still developing. The technology for solar energy economy is already here. The transition to solar systems would create vast numbers of jobs in construction, engineering, and other fields. The politicians have been slow to move toward solar energy because of the power of the corporations. Furthermore, the Departments of Energy and Labor have made no serious effort to look at the employment consequences of energy policies. Traditional energy expansion destroys both jobs and the planet. Only expansion of solar power and conservation guarantee energy supply and jobs for all.

55. El Mallakh, Ragaei. Qatar Energy and Development. New York: St. Martin's Press, 1985.

Qatar is a small oil-producing country in the Arab World, in terms of population and the comparative volume of oil produced annually. The economy depends on oil for 80 percent of its foreign exchange earnings. A large influx of expatriates into Qatar followed the 1973-74 oil price hike. Foreign labor dominates the labor force (85.1%); oil provides about 72% of GDP. In the oil industry, however, nationals constitute more than half of its workforce. Yet, this sector employs only 5 percent of total employment. The high productivity of labor in the petroleum industry is the result of its capital-intensive nature.

Because of the availability of ample reserves of crude oil and natural gas, industries based on these inputs are most likely to be efficient and successful. These industries are both energy and capital intensive. They tend to reduce the total manpower requirements in the economy and assist toward Qatarisation of labor. Within the Qatari oil industry itself, fewer than 2000 persons are employed including the offshore fields. The petrochemical industry provides an example of a capital/energy intensive undertaking. It requires a high capital-labor ratio. Investments per new job is estimated at $20,000 to $100,000. Currently, Qatar lacks adequate trained native manpower. It has to rely on imported labor. The government would like to curtail this long-term dependency and supports the training of indigenous population to fill the jobs.

56. Federal Energy Administration. Labor Report. Project Independence Blueprint Final Task Force Report. Washington, D.C.: U.S. Government Printing Office, November 1974.

The Project Independence Blueprint was designed to address the capability of the United States to achieve relative degrees of energy independence from foreign fuel sources. Nine resource task forces estimated both levels of energy output and resources required to achieve it for the years 1977, 1980, 1985 and 1990. The study recognized constraints in relation to water, labor, material, equipment, finance, transportation and the environment. In particular, the book examines labor in the energy sector and documents the employment trends associated with energy production. Employment in almost every energy industry has declined over the period 1960-1973. Compared to other sectors, employment in energy-production industries showed a higher mix of engineers and blue-collar workers (craftsmen and operators). It is estimated that 70 percent of manpower on oil and gas payrolls require significant lead time for education and training. Furthermore, significant occupational changes have occurred over the past decade in the occupational composition of employment in energy production attributable to the technological changes that have taken place. Employment in the construction of energy facilities is not reported separately. But, based on the pattern of expenditures for energy construction, it appears that employment has expanded significantly. Finally, preliminary estimates of labor required to implement the hypothetical project were made for each energy producing industry (e.g. coal, nuclear power, petroleum, etc.). Their aggregation portrays the overall national labor requirements for Project Independence. The implications of such an implementation would require the attraction of many additional workers into the energy sector, particularly in construction and those geographic areas and occupations where energy employment is concentrated. A labor action program is to facilitate the reallocation process.

57. Fermoselle, Rafael. "Energy and Jobs for the Future," Proceedings of the National Conference on Meeting Energy Workforce Needs, Washington, D.C., February, 1980. Silver Spring, Maryland: Information Dynamics, Inc., 1980, pp. 212-219.

A broad range of energy sources is needed to meet the increasing
demand for energy. The occupational impact of the nation's energy
policies will be different in every state and every region of the
country because of the uneven distribution of every resource
throughout the U.S. This paper reviews the occupational growth of
the different energy resources. Employment in oil and gas industries is expected to increase 70 percent by 1985, and would be
confined to the 10 producing states. There will be an immediate
need for workers for the research and development of synthetic
fuels, as well as for environmental safety and for the operation of
new equipment. The concentration would be in Utah, Colorado, New
Mexico and Wyoming. The development of gasohol would have a
substantial impact on rural areas. Solar technologies are very
labor intensive. The skills required would be in traditional job
categories. Thirty seven states are expected to experience an
increase in mining operations. The number of workers is expected
to rise by 39 percent between 1976 and 1985. Employment in many
states will be affected because of the need to develop a transportation network. Finally, employment at nuclear power plants is
expected to rise in the future. Future growth will depend on
safety and government support.

58. Fitzmaurice, David J. "Perspectives on the United States Energy
Condition: Labor." Paper presented at the National Energy Forum V-A
Sensible Energy Policy Now: Today's Challenge to meet 21st Century
Needs, May 23-24, 1977, Washington, D.C. Sponsored by the U.S. National
Committee of the World Energy Conference, Washington, D.C., pp. 37-39.

This presentation reviews key facts about the U.S. energy condition
and the severity of the problem in terms of projected shortages of
electrical generating capacity, dwindling oil and gas reserves,
nuclear energy potential, conservation, demand for foreign oil and
its balance of payment effects and U.S. foreign policy. It also
highlights the main elements of President Carter proposed energy
plan. It is emphasized, however, that labor cannot accept proposals in terms of conservation that could negatively affect economic
growth. As a representative of the International Union of Electrical Workers, the author reinforces the view of the membership that
it is critical to formulate a national energy plan and to consol-
idate the efforts of labor, business, government, and the public.
Seven specific recommendations are made to that effect. First
price controls oil and natural gas should be maintained. Second,
coal production should be greatly enhanced. Third, nuclear power
need to be expanded. Fourth, the implementation of the energy
program needs to be speeded up. Fifth, there is a definite need
for an extensive R & D program. Sixth, a system of gasoline
rationing should be adopted. Seventh, it is imperative to have
competitive energy industries. So, it appears that the view of
labor supports conservation as an essential but partial solution.
At the same time, the U.S. should rely on its proven reserves of
coal and nuclear energy in the short and middle run.

59. Gallagher, J. Michael and Teather, Jeff S. Availability of Manual
Manpower for U.S. Energy Development Programs. Report prepared by
Bechtel Corporation. Washington, D.C.: U.S. Energy Research and
Development Administration, November 1976. DAE 13794-3 (NTIS)

This report describes the first analysis carried out by Bechtel Corporation for the Energy Research and Development Administration (ERDA) on the subject of the availability of manual manpower for American energy development programs. The intent was to develop information on the availability of manual manpower which could then be used to investigate the feasiblilty of meeting requirements for various energy development programs. Estimates of such requirements are generated by the Energy Supply Planning Model (ESPM) developed by Bechtel for the National Science Foundation and ERDA.

The major results of this study are summaries of the information obtained from senior Bechtel labor relations personnel about the adequacy of manual manpower supplies. This information has also been used to evaluate a set of energy-related requirements.

The findings indicate that (1) as a consequence of the current severe slump in the construction industry, short-term growth requirements could be realized in most regions with few problems, with the exception of highly skilled mechanical crafts (including welders), but that (2) protracted growth at the rates investigated would present substantial problems in meeting requirements for manual manpower and quality field supervision. Historically, the number of building trademen has grown slowly, owing in large part to the long apprenticeship periods required.

What emerges from the above findings is the need for a clear statement of the nation's energy policy which, in turn, would allow enough time for a cooperative effort by labor, government, and industry to ensure that the required building tradesmen are available. An essential ingredient in such a plan should be an energy-related construction program planned over a long period of time (20 to 30 years) so that increases in the supply of construction manpower could be developed for long-term employment. (BC)

60. Gardel, André. Energy Economy and Prospective: A Handbook for Engineers and Economists. Elmsford, New York: Pergamon Press, Inc., 1981.

This publication provides a textbook approach to energy economics. It discusses the consumption and sources of energy; its production, transportation and storage; as well as its costs, both monetary and environmental. Of relevance here is the section on costs. It describes the administrative and personnel costs associated with the operation of various types of electricity plants. An example is given which allows for the determination of the annual personnel charges associated with the operation of a 500 MWE thermal station. It is shown that the total administrative and operating expenses is 2-4 percent of the initial investment. Total costs are estimated as a percentage of investment for this type of plant as well as for nuclear and hydraulic plants. Also given is an estimate of the cost of labor for extraction or collection of coal in France, Germany, the United Kingdom and the United States.

61. Garey, Robert B. and Stevenson, Wayne. Estimated Employment Effects of the Department of Energy's Weatherization Assistance Program. Washington, D.C.: U.S. Department of Energy, March 1983.

The purpose of the Weatherization Assistance Program (WAP) is to conserve energy and reduce the heating bills of low-income families. The program would also provide productive employment to unemployed workers. The study focuses on the number of jobs supported by the program, both for the subgrantee agencies implementing the program and the supporting industries supplying equipment and material. An expenditure of $100 million by subgrantees would create approximately 3600 jobs within the agencies and about 1600 jobs would be created in the supporting agencies. The employment effects were also estimated, subject to varying range of labor intensity and wage rate. To trace the employment effects through a multiplier accounts for some additional 4300 to 5700 jobs induced by the spending of earnings gains enjoyed by those employed workers. The analysis does not estimate the possible losses of employment elsewhere in the economy due to displaced industries. Thus, $100 million expressed in 1983 dollars for WAP would result in the creation of some 10,000 full-time equivalent jobs and this figure does not represent net employment.

62. Goodman, Raymond. "Managing the Demand for Energy in the Developing World," Finance and Development, Vol. 17, No. 4, December 1980, pp. 9-13.

Developing countries consume 12 percent of the world's commercial energy. But, for growth consideration their demand for commercial energy has often outstripped the growth of their GNP. They must import their oil requirements. With using energy costs, oil importing developing countries should expand their own energy resources as well as engage in conservation efforts. If they fail to take positive steps in this direction, their economic growth will slow down. Energy efficiency should represent a principal element of economic planning. Energy demand management becomes a necessity. The pricing policy of energy should reflect its real economic cost (opportunity cost). Government pricing policies need to be corrected accordingly. The article reviews conservation policies in relation to agriculture, industry electric power, and transport. The World Bank experience with industrial projects in the developing countries indicates that substantial energy savings could be achieved in the short run with improved management, personnel training in maintenance, and minor modifications to the existing production processes. In the transport sector, energy savings of 20 to 25 percent are envisaged. For agriculture, rural development strategies should encompass the energy needs of the rural households. Systematic reforestation and the planting of trees on marginal land in cultivated areas need to be undertaken. Many of the measures recommended do not require additional investment. Substantial benefits could be achieved. Such programs may require political decisions and administrative and technical skills which are in short supply in the developing countries. This is where the international community can assist them.

63. Hosni, D. and Sirageldin, I. A Conceptual Framework for Estimating Labor Demand in the Energy Sector of Arab Countries. Safat, Kuwait: Kuwait Institute for Scientific Research (KISR), May 1985.

The growth of the energy sector in the Arab World is highly constrained by shortages of skills (professionals, technicians, and craftsmen). The purpose of this study is to develop a conceptual framework for the estimation of energy labor demand in the Arab countries using the employer survey technique. The estimation stems directly from the corporate plans of the organizations. Based on the current manpower stocks, the forecast would focus on the changes in the energy manning levels needed in the future. The key parameters are turnover and growth. The study outlines the appropriate methodology and presents a case study of Kuwait.

64. Hunt, William D. "Solar Technicians and Mechanics: A Preliminary Occupational Task Analysis." Thesis presented to the faculty of California State University, Chico. Spring 1978.

The study identifies two emerging occupations in the solar heating and cooling industry in California and examines their task requirements. The first occupation is labelled solar mechanic and refers to the performance of mechanical tasks (maintenance and installation of solar equipment). The second is labelled 'solar technician' and refers to the undertaking of quantitative tasks, e.g. sizing, prescribing and designing installation components and systems. The solar occupational analysis was collected through a sample survey of 90 California companies engaged in the installation of solar heating and/or cooling apparatus in building. The reported findings (based on 37 responses) indicate that the companies expect to hire 795 solar mechanics and 208 solar technicians within the next five years, representing an annual growth rate of 34 percent and 25 percent, respectively. Solar technicians were closer to management. Their tasks are not shared by the solar mechanics where as 30 percent of the latter's tasks are shared by the former group. It was concluded that the solar industry in California was not large or mature enough to provide reliable task data. The solar industry, presently unstable, is projected to grow in the near future. The future demand for solar mechanics will exceed that of solar technicians. A more complete manpower analysis of future solar industry is needed at the local, state and national levels.

65. Hunter, Ken. "A Million Man Years of Mining Employment Already Has Been Zapped by Nuclear Power. What Lies Ahead?" United Mine Workers Journal, June, 1978, pp. 4-5.

The article compares the nuclear option to the mining option in terms of their impact on employment. The central argument is that nuclear power plants have wiped out almost a million man years of coal mining employment. At present, there are 70 nuclear reactors with operating licenses. If they were replaced by coal fired power plants, 32,000 more miners would have found employment. The future is dismal for labor when the prospective 141 nuclear plants are actually built. Labor loss is too high. The article reviews the findings of the New Directions publication. The coal strike has triggered renewed interest in nuclear energy declaring coal unreliable. The article quotes the Atomic Industrial forum in that respect. The counterarguments proposed are that 1) nuclear energy destroy rather than create jobs, and 2) produced electricity is not cheap in view of the generous tax-supported subsidies. Coal production requires 40 percent more manpower than nuclear (or more jobs) for each 1,000 megawatt power plant. To go nuclear, therefore, would have drastic negative repercussions to coal miners. The statistics indicate a loss of more than 600 coal mining jobs for every standard size nuclear power plant built. The ratio of coal mine construction to that of nuclear is estimated to be eight to one. For operation and maintenance, coal mining leads ten to one although nuclear is more complex and requires seven steps compared to coal's three steps.

66. International Labour Organization. Assessment of Manpower and Training Requirements in the Energy Sector - The Republic of the Philippines. Geneva: International Labour Organization, 1982. PHI/82 Technical Report.

The successful implementation of a national energy programme requires the support of a system of manpower assessment and planning for the energy sector.The study assesses the manpower and training requirements in the energy sector for the Republic of the Philippines. A manpower survey of all energy agencies and their major contractors was conducted. The questionnaire provided for the collection of data on the current (1982) establishments and vacancies for the projected establishments (1987) and for details on separations over the past year. A major emphasis was placed on developing a list of the principal occupational titles found in the energy sector. The energy sector covered the oil and gas, coal, geothermal, non-conventional fuel, power generation and transmission activities. The principal phases of project activity were identified as a) pre-project activity, b) project management implementation, c) plant construction, and d) plant operation and maintenance. The information provided the basis for estimating manpower demand which was compared to supply to determine the energy manpower and training needs. There is a definite need for an energy manpower system, a standardized information base and the development of an energy manpower planning machinery.

67. International Labour Organization. Major Stages and Steps in Energy Manpower Analysis: A Practical Framework. Geneva: ILO. (In preparation)

Since the oil shocks in the 1970s, efforts have been made in many parts of the world to promote integrated development in the energy sector. Because of a shortage of the necessary skills in developing countries, a plan of action, such as that given in this manual, is needed for building up a pool of skilled manpower to design, implement and monitor effective national energy development programmes and projects. The manual reviews theoretical experience in manpower planning and gives guidelines on its practical application in the energy sector. It covers conventional as well as new and renewable resources, and highlights the special requirements of the household energy sector. (ILO)

68. Institute of Nuclear Power Operations. Training and Education Division. 1982 Survey of Nuclear-Related Occupational Employment in the United States Electric Utilities. Atlanta, Georgia: Institute of Nuclear Power Operations, December 1982. INPO 82-031

This is a report of a survey of nuclear-related occupational employment in selected management, professional, and technical positions in the United States Electric Utilities. By the same token, the current status of nuclear-related training in the utilities is examined. Information was collected on 1) on-site and off-site nuclear employments in March 1982, 2) number of vacancies in March 1982, 3) projected employment levels for the period 1982-1991, and 4) turnover data for 1981. There were 45,920 nuclear-related positions (management, professional, and technical). The percentage of vacancies was calculated to be 12.5. The turnover data showed that 5.4 percent of employees left the positions. The projected figure for growth was 7.3 percent for 1982-1991. Based on such data, the nuclear utilities needed 31,119 additional employees during the period under study. The study details the information by type of job. The occupational classification is for managers and supervisors, engineers (by type), scientists (by type), training personnel (by type), operators, and technical and maintenance personnel. Wide variations are reported. Training efforts need to be directed to the following occupations: licensed operators, senior licensed operators, relation protection technicians, and instrument control technicians. Finally, the findings of the 1982 survey are compared to the 1981 data or the first survey of occupational employment.

69. Kramer Associates, Inc. Determination of Labor Management in the Bituminous Coal Industry to meet the Goals of Project Independence. Washington, D.C.: Kramer and Associates, Inc., September 8, 1977.

This report uses Project Independence's 1985 production target of 1100 million tons of bituminous coal to determine the manpower requirements for the industry. The 1970's have been characterized by an expansion of employment in the bituminous coal industry due to sharp declines in productivity in the underground mines and little improvement in the productivity in surface mining. It is projected for 1976-1977, however, that productivity will reach an annual rate of 2.5 percent in underground and 3.0 percent in surface. Combining this productivity estimate with the 1985 production target suggests 182,000 workers will be employed in underground mines and 73,100 in surface mines in 1985. This total of 255,000 is an increase over 1974 of 87,600 workers or 53 percent. In addition to the manpower requirements for expanding production, the coal industry must also account for retirements and replacements to obtain the total manpower needs. In a total requirement of 144,100 workers over the 11 year period, slightly over 60% will be for expansion and 40% for replacement. This study also addresses the characteristics of the additional labor force for recruitment and training purposes. The analysis shows that some occupations will grow faster than others. The mechanics-repair-maintenance category is expected to increase in proportion to total employment. Engineers are expected to show substantial growth with the opening of new mines. Because of increased technology, cutting and drilling machine operators will experience a lower than average growth. Improvements in coal haulage systems are causing a decline in the need for shuttle car operators and motormen. Heavy machine operators in surface mining are expected to experience more than average growth. There are many more educational and training opportunities in underground than in surface mining. Training would vary among companies and areas.

70.   Kramer   Associates,   Inc.   Energy   Manpower   Fact   Book,   1981. Washington,   D.C.:   U.S.   Department   of   Energy,   December   1981. DOE/IR/06647-1 (NTIS)

This report presents statistical data about manpower engaged in the development, production and distribution of energy. It is the first compilation of a factbook about the utilization of energy manpower. The sources of energy include: coal mining, oil and gas extraction, petroleum refining, solar energy, geothermal energy, electric and gas utilities. For each source employment trends, employment by occupation, labor supply and training, hours, earnings and labor turnover, technological changes and productivity, safety and industrial hazards are reported. The appendix offers the statistical supporting data.

71. Kramer Associates Inc. Manpower Requirements and Availability for Projected Coal Production in Ten Eastern States to 1985. Final report submitted to the Federal Energy Administration, September 8, 1977. Washington, D.C.: U.S. Department of Energy, September 1977.

The projections of the Federal Energy Administration are used to determine the manpower required by the bituminous coal industry for the year 1985 for 10 states east of the Mississippi River. The 10 states studied are: Pennsylvania, Ohio, Maryland, West Virginia, Alabama, Virginia, Tennessee, Kentucky, Illinois and Indiana.

Using the productivity factor of output of coal per man-year of labor, West Virginia shows the greatest discrepancy between the manpower needed by 1985 and that which is estimated to be available.   This is occurring despite competitive wage rates.   West Virginia's geographic location has resulted in a smaller labor pool than other states. A deficit of 86,230 miners is predicted. East Kentucky will have small shortages through 1985 but major problems are not expected. Migration rates are very high and increasing at a constant rate. There is no surplus labor, however, to spill into West Virginia. West Kentucky and Illinois, despite their decreasing population, have sufficient labor and are not expected to have any problems. Pennsylvania has a large labor pool, with population growing in the coal areas. It shows a small but insignificant deficit by 1985. It is suggested that West Virginia must find a way to encourage miners from Tennessee, Virginia and Ohio the move into the area or they will not be able to meet the manpower requirements for projected production goals. The number of workers needed to mine future coal production is largely determined by the productivity trends in the future. There is a high range of variability in coal mine productivity among the different states and local coal fields. The greatest diversity is between underground and surface mining. The latter has shown a relatively higher productivity over the past year. In converting output of coal into manpower requirements, it is important to keep track of a) output of average mines per man-hour or man-day and b) number of days worked per year. There are wide ranges in these two factors among the ten states under study.

72. Korba, Aziz Amara. "The Significance of Engineering in the Economic Development of the Arab World." Paper presented at the Third Arab Energy Conference - Energy and Cooperation, May 4-9, 1985. Safat, Kuwait: OAPEC, 1985.

The engineering share of the OAPEC oil and gas sector has significantly increased over the last decade from 10 million to 20 million man-hours per year. The Arab companies' share was only 100,000 man-hours per year. There is a definite lack of significant Arab engineering capabilities with serious consequences on the economies of the Arab States. The greatest concern is that approximately 70 percent of an engineering company's income goes to the home country in Europe and North America.

These facts suggest that the Arab world must develop its own engineering talents. Engineers must receive the level of respect that they experience in the developed countries. Also, Arab engineering and financial institutions must be encouraged and assisted in this development effort. The principal requirements needed to form Arab engineering companies are:

1. Sufficient numbers of top professional managers and engineers are needed. These must be recruited from Europe or North America, if necessary.

2. A high level of commitment must be achieved in order to develop a company of substantial size with the essential human and technological resources.

3. A high initial investment.

4. Reduced geographic, industrial and technological barriers so that the newly acquired capability can be sold everywhere.

5. International competition in order to maintain internal discipline and encourage entrepreneurial qualities.

6. Active support from the home market.

This discussion shows that the means exist for growth in the Arab engineering capability and the case for creating this growth is overwhelming.

73. Levy, Girard W. and Field, Jennifer. Solar Energy Employment and Requirement 1978-1985: Summary and Highlights. Washington, D.C.: U.S. Department of Energy, April 1980. DOE ITIC-1154

The objective of this study is to collect data on employment by occupation, to analyze the education and experience of solar energy personnel, and to project the future manpower requirements through 1983. The study focused on professional, technical, and skilled craft occupations. All types of employees and of solar technologies as well as all stages of work are covered by the study. The study describes the methodology of the development of a survey questionnaire. A mail questionnaire was sent to 2800 establishments and another for 500 employees working in solar energy. A total of 1314 establishments responded. A total of 563 establishments were engaged in solar activities and five states show the most solar concentration (California, New York, Massachusetts, Colorado and Texas). The percentage of employees engaged in solar work varied inversely with the size of establishments. Small establishments concentrated on installation and engineering services whereas large organizations were more involved in R & D work (75%). In 1978, it was estimated that 22,500 persons were working in solar energy. More employees were associated with R & D than commercial and installation activities. High gains in employment were anticipated, mostly for skilled workers and technicians. New skills were identified with solar design and installation. The employment levels are expected to triple by 1983. Most of the increase is with commercial solar energy. Employment in R & D is also projected to increase.

The existing solar manpower is underutilized as evidenced by the number of hours worked (30 hours). The employees reported the need for more education and training. The study offers several recommendations to improve the solar manpower data as well as the projections.

74. "Manpower Gap at Uranium Mines," Business Week, November 7, 1977, p. 32.

The U. S. Uranium companies are experiencing a serious shortage in manpower despite their wages of $20,000 to $50,000 a year. The working conditions are too demanding and uncomfortable to attract and keep workers. This problem is compounded by the fact that the industry needs to gear up to triple its annual production in order to meet the increasing demands of the nuclear fuel industry. This article explains that there are only 4,100 uranium miners now working but that 22,400 will be needed by 1990.

To get the needed manpower, companies must train their miners from scratch. This costs the companies approximately $80,000 per miner. In an effort to trim these costs, one company is training Navajo Indians with the Labor Department financing the $2 million program. It is hoped that this program will alleviate the tribe's chronic unemployment of 40 percent as well as help the uranium industry with its manpower shortage.

75. Mendis, Matthew S.; Rosenberg, Joseph I.; Medville, Douglas M.; Stokes, Betsy A.; Reirson, James D.; and Cumiskey, Patricia L. Manpower for the Coal Mining Industry: An Assessment of Adequacy through the year 2000. McClean, Virginia: The MITRE Corporation, March 1980.

The study examines the various aspects of the manpower supply and demand outlook of the coal mining industry through the year 2000. The econometric model developed centers on three sectors: labor demand, labor supply and wage determination. The model incorporates key variables as labor productivity, coal production, technological mix and capital costs. The objective is to estimate imbalances between labor supply and demand by producing area, mining technology and skill category. The range of probable

employment futures developed in association with three coal demand
scenarios were assessed in light of expected industry trends and
conditions.

Study results indicate that there will be sufficient professional
manpower supplies in general. The inexperienced workers group
shows the greatest variance among the employment futures. Mining
technicians represent the fastest growing component of the coal
industry workforce (15% per year and their share of total coal
industry personnel is expected to increase from 1 percent in 1980
to over 5 percent by year 2000. Periodic shortages of experienced
hourly production workers, especially in the Northern Great Plains,
can be expected. Area surface mining is anticipated to dominate
coal production by the year 2000. This would reduce the share of
mining engineers modestly. The study findings support the unlike-
lihood of shortages of mining engineers. It points out, however,
to the difficulty of attracting mining and mineral engineering
faculty whose salaries are low relative to those paid by industry.
Labor productivity in deep surface mining is likely to increase
moderately in the 80's. Finally, the study provides several
recommendations to the federal government in terms of implementing
manpower and training programs and to the academic community for
appropriate program emphasis based on the industry future needs.

76. Morgenstern, R.D. and Vroman, W. Energy Conservation and the Demand
for Labour: Evidence from Aggregate Data. Washington, D.C.: The Urban
Institute, May 1981.

This study seeks to explore the relationship between aggregate
employment and output, with special reference to the doubling of
oil prices in 1979 and the significant rise in unemployment in
1980. It was hypothesized that an indirect relationship exists
between the energy price shocks and the occupational mix. Specifically, the energy price shocks of 1978-1979 may have created new
opportunities for short-term energy conservation investments which,
in turn, increased the demand for blue collar labor. The basic
hypothesis is tested by estimating a time series model of occupational industrial employment patterns which included a set of
variables to measure price shocks. The energy price variables were
only mildly significant, adding little to the explanatory power of
the equations. The conclusion was that it was not possible to
discern a consistent and statistically significant relationship
between the recent energy price shocks and employment patterns.

77. Nielsen, George F. "Coal Mine Development and Expansion
Survey...617.3 Million Tons of New Capacity 1977 Through 1985,"
Coal Age, February 1977, pp. 83-100.

The Keystone Coal Industry Manual reports coal mine development and
expansion plans between 1977 and 1985. An estimated 617.3 million
tons of new capacity are reported bringing the total output of 315
mines surveyed to about 777.5 millions tons of coal. The survey
covered twenty-one states. Strip mining dominates underground
mining. Surface mining will account for about 65.4 percent of new
capacity and will cover log mines. The greatest amount of capacity
is expected to be associated with Wyoming, followed by Montana,

Utah, and North Dakota. The figures reported do not reflect the amount of replacement tonnage. The article presents five detailed statistical tables reflecting on the expansion of new coal mines by number, type, capacity, and location covering a nine year period. The employment potential of such an expansion deserves serious consideration.

78. Nordlund, Willis J. and Mumford, John. "Estimating Employment Potential in U.S. Energy Industries," Monthly Labor Review, May 1978, pp. 12-13.

It is maintained that reliance on domestic energy sources would promote more employment in U.S. energy industries. Coal mining and power plant construction would provide most of the new job opportunities. The bulk of the new job openings will be filled by the unemployed. Three occupational requirements for power plant construction are identified with more than 100,000 workyears (pipefitters, laborers, and electricians) covering 47 percent of the construction workforce. The forecasts are estimated using the construction Manpower Demand System (CMDS). Increased demand for coal is expected for the next two or three decades. Expanded coal production has already increased job opportunities in the last few years. Estimates are based on industry reports on size, location and timing of mining development. But two important manpower problems plague the industry. First, productivity declines (especially with underground mining) have been experienced. Several factors explain this phenomenon and include a younger and inexperienced workforce, tougher health and safety rules and, more frequent strikes. Second, coalmining (underground) is not appealing to new workforce members. At the same level of productivity, additional employment of over 200,000 miners is expected. The total direct employment from power plant construction and coal mining is estimated at 175,000 workyears annually. The secondary employment may be large - based on a multiplier of 1.5 to 2.5 this is, particularly so, with coal mining.

79. Nordlund, Willis J. and Robson, R. Thayne. Energy and Employment. New York: Praeger Publishers, 1980.

The book highlights the employment dimension of the energy problems and solutions. It gives an overview of employment in the energy sector. It examines energy as a factor of production in the production/consumption process. It identifies employment in coal and electricity and the jobs associated with solar energy. The socioeconomic impact of energy development is assessed. Different energy-employment analytical models are reviewed. Finally, specific macro and micro policy recommendations are offered as well as an agenda for future research.

80. Pereira, Armand. "Employment Implications of Ethanol Production in Brazil," International Labor Review, Vol. 122, No.1, January-February 1983, pp. 111-127.

As a result of the oil crisis and the rising oil prices, Brazil shifted to alcohol as a substitute for gasoline. An ambitious national alcohol programme has been introduced to reduce the

country's dependence on oil imports, whereby 85 percent of requirements are imported. The ethanol programme depends on heavy public
subsidies. Its direct employment impact is positive. The paper
discusses the methodology of employment assessment, the direct
impact of individual ethanol distilleries and of total ethanol
production as well as the qualitative aspects of direct as employment, including seasonality. It was found out that the mix of
permanent and seasonal workers varies significantly from one
plantation to another. The data used were based partly on field
surveys supplemented by published information and interviews with
public officials and managers of distilleries and plantations. In
1980, about 15,939 man-year jobs and 6,417 seasonal jobs of 150
days have been created in administrative/agri-industrial activities. It is estimated that the total work force employed under
this program in 1980 amounts to about 40,000 and 82,000 permanent
and seasonal workers during the harvest and off-seasons. These
benefits must be weighed against the employment implications of
substitution of crop and pastures. The displacement, however,
implies a net gain of 24,400 man-years of employment because
sugar-cane is more labor-intensive. It is important, however, not
to ignore the side-effects (low income, using concentration of land
ownership). Policy efforts should be directed at providing more
stable employment and improving the real incomes of the present
work force.

81. Quick, Allen H. and Buck, Neal A. Strategic Planning for
Exploration Management. Boston, Massachusetts: International Human
Resources Development Corporation, 1983.

This book provides an understanding of the strategic planning
process that should be used to run exploration operations as
business units. Portfolio analysis, econometric and planning
techniques are presented in direct application to exploration
management. Using the process described will aid in the prediction
of growth potential, revenue increases, and production cost increases, including employment requirements.

82. Rodberg, Leonard S. "Jobs: The Employment Opportunity in
Renewable Energy," Sun Times, May/June, 1983, pp. 3-5.

The fields of energy conservation and renewable energy offers a
good opportunity for the structurally unemployed. The renewable
energy industry could contribute about 20 percent of the nation's
energy by year 2000 and might employ about 1.4 million people.
Different studies and projects have demonstrated the potential for
useful employment in solar energy. The demand for conservation and
solar installations, however, have grown slowly due to cost,
unfamiliarity and public misinformation. Aggressive steps need to
be taken to overcome this reluctance. Firms engaged in renewable
energy work tend to be small and widely spread throughout the
country. The capital requirements to join the industry are modest.
About half of the jobs in solar energy would be accessible to
workers with no prior training supplemented by one-year of on-the-
job training. Finally these programs would have great potential
for community economic development.

83. Rosenthal, Neal H.   "The Future Workforce Requirements in Energy Producing Industries," Proceedings of the National Conference on Meeting Energy Workforce Needs, Washington, D.C., February, 1980. Silver Spring, Maryland: Information Dynamics, Inc., 1980, pp. 22-27.

Employment trends in energy producing industries have declined in the 50's and 60's and recently picked up again. Different energy producing industries reflect different growth patterns. Each of the industries, moreover, depicts a different occupational structure that relates to its own activities. The share of engineers and scientists in the industry's total employment ranges from one percent (coal mining) to five percent (crude petroleum and natural gas extraction). By the same token operations make up about 50 percent of total employment economy in 1990, future projections indicate an increase of 13.5 percent. The highest growth share (50%) is associated with coal mining. The number of miners demanded is expected to grow rapidly and could present a potential manpower dilemma. For the other energy producing industries, growth is just moderate.

84. Rungeling, Brian; Smith, Lewis H.; Smith, James O. Jr.; Boyet, Wayne E.; and Willenoes, Rhonda. Labor Force Study for the Yellow Creek Project. University, Mississippi: The University of Mississippi, Center for Manpower Studies, March 31, 1977.

This report assesses the availability of local labor for the construction of the Yellow Creek Project planned by TVA in Northeast Mississippi. The supply of skilled craftsmen was estimated under various assumptions. First, assuming an open competitive labor market (open shop), a shortage of workers in seven skill crafts is anticipated in 1982. Second, assuming an institutionally restricted labor market (hiring hall), deficits in several skill categories are anticipated. For every one percent wage differential the supply of craftsmen available to TVA will expand by one percent from within the commuting area (based on a fifty mile radius). The deficits would be alleviated by the training of local workers as opposed to the attraction of outside workers. The union apprenticeship program of local unions could be, in part, used for this purpose. TVA must provide the necessary fundings. The adverse long-run impact after project completion in terms of trained persons are minimal. Several recommendations were made to institute the training of workers to alleviate the labor shortages at Yellow Creek.

85. Short, John; Harris, Jeffrey; Waldo, Judith; and Barber, Sharla. A Study to Determine the Manpower and Training Needs of the Coal Mining Industry. Washington, DC: U.S. Department of the Interior, Dec. 1979. PB80-164742 (NTIS)

The projected rapid development of coal production in the U.S. led to an evaluation of the training needs of the industry. Coal mining employment is projected to experience a 100 percent increase by 1995. The assessment of future demand for safety training and supervisory maintenance and production skills development depends on the flow of individuals in and out of the industry and on the transition of miners through the various occupations. An Employment/Turnover Model generates the estimates of training incidences by region and type of mining for any production/productivity assumptions. The study presents a profile of the existing and future coal mine work force. For the future, the coal mine work force is expected to be younger, better educated, drawn from non-mine related occupations and relatively immobile. The study presents a region by region analysis of the forecast of the coal mine work force. A review of the various training provided, reveals that the system lacks effective coordination among them (coal companies, schools, state and federal government, equipment manufacturers, consultants, trade associations, and unions). Several recommendations were made concerning the future role of the federal government in assuring the availability of an adequately trained coal mine work force. They range from the creation of mining extension service and resource centers to the provision of tax incentives for the development and implementation of more effective/ efficient training methods, as well as the formation of a federal interagency committee.

86. The Solar Work Institute. The Solar Work Survey: A Status Report on California's Solar Collector Industry. Sacramento, California: State of California, Office of the Governor, 1982.

Solar energy will provide jobs and economic growth of significant scale. This is based on a solar work survey in relation to California's solar collector industry. About 7000 firms are engaged in solar activities in California. The industry is seasonal and the demand is highest by the fourth quarter of calendar year for tax credit purposes. Most installers are trained on-the-job. The structure of the solar industry is made up of small businesses (14 employees on average). Business leaders in the survey were optimistic about the industry growth over the next decade based on a continued solar tax credit system and a prospering general economy. The survey provides updated information in terms of size, dollars, locations and number of years in operation. Job title descriptions, modes of payment and pay structure are described. The survey reviews recruitment, training and employment practices.

87. State of California, Employment Development Department. Employment and Training in California's Energy Sector. Sacramento, California: State of California, Employment Development Department, 1980.

This report describes direct employment in California's energy sector at the present time and for the near future. For policy purposes, the employment impact of specific energy programs is an important consideration to determine the choice of future energy systems. It is necessary, therefore, to keep up with the demand for and the supply of labor in terms of both numbers and skill levels. Average annual employment estimates by occupation are presented for each industry category of the energy sector in California covering conventional and alternative energy production as well as conservation. California's energy sector's share of the total state workforce is very small (slightly above one percent). The bulk of employment is in conventional industries. However, it is expected that the alternative and conservation technologies

would depict a higher rate of growth in employment in the near
future (predominantly within the active solar subsector). The
occupational pattern indicates higher proportions of professional,
technical, and skilled craft workers relative to the statewide one.
The details of the occupational mix and geographic distribution are
provided. The report also reviews the state inventory of training
programs in energy-related occupations in order to identify
training gaps. The findings here are tentative because of data
limitations. The major policy conclusion supported by the findings
indicates that direct employment impacts should be regarded as a
minor consideration in the choice of energy options, at least for
the near future.

88. State of Colorado. Department of Labor and Employment. Energy
Employment and Training Needs Task Force. A Report to the Governor on
Energy Employment and Training Needs in Colorado 1980-2000. Denver,
Colorado: Colorado Department of Labor 1980.

This report discusses the development of an adequate labor force to
meet the energy needs of Colorado for the next two decades. The
report reviews the impact of energy development on the workforce
(present and future). The current employment estimates are based
on the latest employer data for coal mining, oil and gas, and oil
shale. The energy occupational employment are presented for mining
and construction in 1980 and 1990. The capacity of the education
and training systems is evaluated. There is a critical need for
facilities expansion and their modernization. Demand (jobs) and
supply (students) in the four planning regions are evaluated.
There is a potential short fall of workers in the energy impact
areas by year 1990. Colorado would like to improve the matching of
state unemployed workers to energy development jobs and to minimize
in migration. The report explores the alternative means of meeting
labor force needs. The following measures are recommended: 1) to
improve the use of existing energy work force, 2) to increase
labor force participation, 3) to encourage intra-state migration
from high unemployment areas to the energy sector, 4) to facilitate
in-state migration, 5) to increase the output of vocational
training, and 6) to develop a backup strategy for the possible
importation of Labor.

89. Third Arab Energy Conference. "Country Paper - Republic of
Lebanon." Paper presented at the Third Arab Energy Conference - Energy
and Cooperation, May 4-9, 1985, Algiers, Algeria. Safat, Kuwait:
OAPEC, 1985.

The paper reviews the consumption patterns, energy sources, pricing
and investment requirements in the Republic of Lebanon. The
economic conditions as they relate to energy are examined. In the
area of manpower, 536 refiners and technicians are employed in the
oil sector and the appointment of 196 new employees are forecasted.
Currently, the electricity sector employs 3,177 technical people
with a forecast of 1,269 people to be employed. (OAPEC)

90. Turner, Brian and Lav, Iris J. Energy for a Working America.
Washington, D.C.: Industrial Union Department, AFL-CIO, April 1980.

This is a comprehensive look at the energy problems. Different issues are addressed: pricing and inflation, jobs, ownership, environment, safety and health, etc. It explains the range of energy technologies to solve the energy problems. The focus is on: conservation, electrical generating capacity, synthetic liquid fuels and gas, and renewable sources like solar and gasohol. The most important impact of energy on jobs will be in specific industries and specific groups of unemployed workers. For example, it is estimated that 70 to 80 percent of all the jobs associated with weatherization, for instance, are unskilled. Increasing energy efficiency in residential and commercial establishments is expected to add 200,000 jobs widely distributed throughout the country. Solar energy applications are expected to provide as many as 400,000 new jobs by 1990. There might also be an addition of 100,000 jobs in coal mining, 150,000 construction jobs in power plant construction, and 280,000 jobs in the construction of synthetic fuel plants. A total of approximately 1.1 million new jobs by 1990 is predicted and it is expected that the unemployment rate drop by one percent by 1990. The study recommends that these options be implemented in the eighties to free American from reliance on foreign oil.

91. U.K. Department of Employment. Manpower Requirements of the Energy Industries. Energy Commission Paper, No. 18. London, U.K.: U.K. Department of Employment, 1978. ISSN 0140-7996

This paper investigates the effects of manpower constraints on the orderly and successful exploitation of energy resources over the medium term. It is mainly concerned with the energy producing industries themselves with a workforce of 650,000 workers. In general, there seems to be no problem with the recruitment of university, professional and technical groups. There is, however, a problem of shortage of engineers and technologists that needs to be addressed. There is no potential problem with the recruitment and retention of skilled or unskilled workers. It is important, however, to maintain systematic manpower planning and to improve the training system. The manpower structures of the individual energy industries are presented with special emphasis on their future manpower requirements.

92. United Nations Conference on Trade and Development. The Energy Sector in Developing Countries: Issues in the Transfer, Application and Development of Technology. New York: United Nations, August 19, 1982.

The present study examines the issues of transfer, applicability and development of energy technology in developing countries. It is divided into three parts. A review of the energy situation of the developing countries provides a background for the discussion of issues. The second part analyzes issues related to each of the main energy technologies (petroleum exploration, power plant procurement, development and diffusion of new/renewable sources of energy). The planning and management of the power sector calls for the broad range of skills and capabilities. The same applies to power plant operating technology, including troubleshooting capability for repair. Managerial and technological expertise is needed to organize and decide on oil exploration and development programmes. By the same token, oil field skills are needed for project implementation. So, a domestic national expertise is needed to plan, carry, and manage the entire energy sector. Government plays a central role in relation to that sector. As the developing countries need for technical assistance and cooperation will be expanding rapidly the relevant organizations (Advisory Service on Transfer of Technology UNCTAD) should be able to respond to their growing requests. Part three examines the areas where a comprehensive framework for action at national, regional, and international levels could be formulated.

93. U. S. Bureau of Labor Statistics. "Occupations in the Atomic Energy Field," Occupational Outlook Handbook. Washington, D.C.: Department of Labor, 1976, pp. 613-620.

This paper discusses how atomic energy is produced. It also reviews the nature of the atomic energy field. The Federal Government supports over half of the basic atomic energy activities. The U.S. Energy Research and Development Administration (ERDA) directs the Government's research program. The Nuclear Regulatory Commission (NRC) controls the case of nuclear materials by private organizations. About 50 percent of all workers in the atomic energy field are employed by government-owned facilities. Because much of the work is in the stage of research and development, engineers scientists, technicians and craft workers dominate the manpower structure. The paper undertakes to list the different activities of the atomic energy field and the corresponding workers involved in 1974. The article also points out to the unique occupations associated with atomic energy (e.g. health physicists, radiation chemist, nuclear reactor operator, radiation, monitor, etc.). Training plays an important role in the atomic energy field. About one-fourth of the scientists and engineers in ERDA hold a PhD degree. Skill requirements for craft workers in the atomic energy field is above that of most industries because of the precision requirements. Government contractors offer training at their own plants or with nearby institutions. It is maintained that employment in the atomic energy field is expected to grow much faster than the average for all industries. This will be brought about by the expansion of the nuclear generating capacity and increases in R & D expenditures. The hourly earnings of blue-collar workers in the atomic field are higher than those of all manufacturing industries. Extensive safeguards protect the health and safety of workers in that field. Most hourly paid plant workers are organized.

94. U.S. Department of Energy. Office of Energy Research. Manpower Assessment Programs. Energy-Related Manpower, 1983. Washington, D.C.: U.S. Department of Energy, November 1983.

The purpose of this report is to discuss the employment requirements and manpower supply implications of projected trends in energy R & D and energy production activities for 1983 through 1988. An overview of recent energy trends and their implications for employment of scientists, engineers and related workers is given. The supply of qualified personnel needed to perform energy-related activities and its adequacy is discussed. Additionally, a summary review of 10 recent studies addressing the current efforts to identify employment and training in various energy areas is offered.

The estimates in this report primarily come from a survey of employers which was conducted by the Department of Labor's Bureau of Labor Statistics. The 1983 employment was the base for the report and provides estimates of employment changes for 1984 and 1988. It is stated that demand for energy-related manpower is sensitive to changes in energy production levels. Trends indicate that energy production is expected to increase moderately through 1988. The trends, however vary with energy source. The following energy categories are examined: oil and gas, nuclear, coal, and conservation and renewables. Many employers expect demand to increase in several areas. In fact, some shortages are anticipated, especially in the field of engineering.

95. U.S. Department of Energy. Office of Energy Research. Office of Field Operations Management. Geothermal Energy Employment and Requirements 1977-1990. Washington, D.C.: U.S. Department of Energy, December 1981. DOE/IRI 70004-1 (NTIS)

This report assesses the manpower needs of the geothermal industry. The specific objectives include 1) a base line estimation of geothermal manpower, 2) likelihood of skill shortages, 3) future employment, and 4) recommendations for meeting manpower requirements. Interviews and mail surveys indicate an estimated employment equivalent of 3,340 full-time persons in 1977 working for about 697 organizations (private public and educational establishments). There is a high concentration as 52 percent of the reported employment is associated with the twenty largest employers. R & D manpower involvement is estimated to be 25.8 percent. Scientists and engineers share is significantly high (60 %). The study identifies the occupations that are currently or are expected to be constraints on industry growth (geologists, geophysicists, reservoir and environmental engineers and drilling personnel. The problem relates to lack of geothermal courses curricula. Manpower forecasts are carried for the segment of industry covering electrical energy production. The minimum (11,802) and maximum (32,339) in 1985 and minimum (37,073) and maximum (101,000) for 1990 are given. The maximum employment growth scenario will not have a significant national impact. The suggested alternatives include: financial support to expand geothermal curricula; periodic mail surveys to keep track of industry evolution; and the development of a rationalized manpower information system for the energy industries.

3
Energy-Employment Models

96. Bailey, James E. "Energy, Labor and Capital Considerations in Productivity Enhancements," in J.E. Bailey (editor). Energy Systems: An Analysis for Engineers and Policy Makers. New York: Marcel Dekker, 1978.

This paper questions our concepts of productivity enhancement in an era where energy is neither cheap nor reliable. The central issue is: "Can we still afford to enhance productivity by substituting energy for capital and labor and then require that the production system support those people in non-productive activities?" A model of the production system is presented which considers labor, capital and the energy concerns. It is suggested that the industrial and management engineering communities be encouraged to conserve natural resources through increased employment of labor. The author suggests that regulations and incentives to encourage more low-wage jobs will reduce the demand for energy.

97. Bezdek, Roger H. Long-Range Forecasting of Manpower Requirements: Theory and Applications. New York: Manpower Planning Committee, Institute of Electrical and Electronics Engineers, Inc., 1974.

This extensive work discusses the importance of optimal manpower policies in economic plans. It describes several different methods of forecasting manpower requirements. The author develops a basic systematic model and applies it to several forecasting situations. Of particular interest is the application of a modified version of the Center for Advanced Computation (CAC) manpower forecasting model. This involves an investigation of the effects on employment and energy requirements which might result if the Federal highway trust fund expenditures are allocated to other programs, such as mass transit development. The empirical results show that total employment requirements would increase and total energy requirements would decrease if the highway trust funds were diverted from highway construction to other federal programs. The aggregate employment shifts are broken down into net effects upon demand for specific occupations, jobs, and level of skill. Also, it shows that certain occupations stand to gain

at the expense of others. The net impact depends on the alternate
types of programs which are funded.

98. Bezdek, Roger and Hannon, Bruce. "Energy, Manpower, and the
Highway Trust Fund," Science, Vol. 185, No. 4152, August 23, 1974, pp.
669-675.

Energy conservation could be achieved by reinvesting the highway
trust fund into alternative federal programs. This article
computes the net impacts on energy consumption and manpower that
would result from reallocating the $5 billion highway trust fund
to other federal programs like railroad and mass transit development, educational facilities construction, water and waste
treatment facilities, law enforcement, national health insurance
and tax relief programs. This is done using the energy-manpower
policy simulation model prepared by the Center for Advanced
Computation (CAC) for each program. The simulation showed the $5
billion are to be translated into direct and indirect occupational
requirements. Each program generates higher total labor requirements and is less energy demanding. The aggregate employment
shifts are broken into the net effects upon demand for specific
occupations, numbers of jobs and levels of skills. A comparison of
highway transportation with railroad transportation in terms of
dollar, energy, and employment needs is undertaken. Specific
comparisons are made between passenger and freight transport and
railroad to support the savings in energy and the increase in
employment.

99. Brooks, W.; Cachart, S.C.; McGranahan, G.O.; and Mulherkar, S.S.
Energy and Economic Evaluation of Policies for Accelerated Investment in
Efficient Automobiles. Washington, D.C.: U.S. Department of Energy,
August 1978. BNL-50901 (NTIS)

This report examines the effect of an energy-conservation policy
that imposes excise taxes on cars having low fuel efficiency,
coupled with a rebate on cars having high fuel efficiency. Two oil
price cases are considered. The Jack Faucett Automobile Sector
Forecasting Model is used to measure direct effects. The
Brookhaven National Laboratory - University of Illinois Input-
Output/Linear Programming Model is used for economy-wide effects
and impact on employment. (NTIS)

100. Cohn, Elcharan; Nelson, Jon P.; Neumann, George R.; Lewis, Morgan
V.; and Kaufman, Jacob J. The Bituminous Coal Industry: A Forecast.
University Park: Pennsylvania State University, 1975.

This study develops an econometric model to forecast the demand
for and supply of manpower in the bituminous coal industry in the
years 1985 and 2000. It is divided into three parts. First, the
study gives an overview of the energy market and summarizes the
government policies pertinent to safety, health and the environment. The location, costs and labor productivity of coal mining,
as well as mining technology development are examined. The study
also offers a profile of the mine worker. Second, the manpower
forecasting techniques are evaluated and the methodology adopted
is outlined. Total regional and selected state manpower demand
and supply forecasts are given. It is not likely that there will

be national shortage of labor in the coal industry. The possibility of regional shortages and surpluses is envisaged. A shift
of coal production to the West is considered with surface mining.
A new set of skills will be needed than presently being used in the
East. It is recommended that the U.S. Bureau of Mines undergo
periodic evaluation of manpower forecasts.

101. Construction Manpower Demand System. General Plan of Development.
Washington, D.C.: U.S. Department of Labor, August, 1977.

This study concentrates on the construction sector which
contributes 70 percent of GNP with an annual employment share of 5
percent. The characteristics of this sector are : fragmented,
organization by work function, floating labor pool, and
intermittent (cyclical and seasonal) employment. This publication
focuses on the development of a comprehensive information system
known as Construction Manpower Demand System (CMDS) to provide
current and future construction data as well as the corresponding
labor requirements of construction activity. The system is
developed in two phases. Phase I provides for an automated or data
base system on the construction activity and related labor demand
projections. Phase II deals with forecasting construction by
region and its manpower requirements. This will improve planning
and enhance the utilization of labor in construction. The
potential users of this system include the Federal Government
agencies, state and government bodies, and the private sector. In
particular, the Federal Energy Administration (FEA), the Energy
Research and Development Administration (ERDA), and the Tennessee
Valley Authority (TVA). Such agencies require information by
specific type of energy-related construction, e.g. hydroelectric
power plant construction, as well as by geographical distribution.
The new Department of Energy (DOE) will use the system to gain
insight into the regional impact of energy development on the
construction industry and its labor force. This would provide the
basis for evaluating alternative energy development plans. As such
it would represent the human resources input to national energy
planning. The TVA builds its own generation facilities.
Construction labor costs represents about 30 percent of total cost
of a nuclear generating station. Electricity rates are, therefore,
tied to the labor bill. TVA could identify craft bottlenecks and
undertake intensified training and recruitment in those areas to
alleviate such constraints. TVA can assist CETA sponsors by
providing job opening information in relation to manpower planning
and training. The CMDS is highly useful and needed.

102. Denny, Michael and Fuss, Melvyn. "The Effects of Factor Prices and
Technological Change on the Occupational Demand for Labor: Evidence
from Canadian Telecommunications," The Journal of Human Resources,
XVII, 2, 1983, pp. 161-176.

This paper investigates the effect of automation on the occupational demand for labor using modern econometric demand theory.
We are able to estimate labor demand functions derived from a
production process characterized by variable elasticities of
substitution, nonhomothetic output expansion effects, and
non-neutral technical change. The model is applied to a large

Canadian telecommunications firm, Bell Canada, for the period 1952-1972 when detailed data on four occupational groups, capital, materials, output, and the extent of automation are available. The empirical results demonstrate the strong effects of innovative activity in this industry. Technical change was capital-using and labor-saving, with the labor-saving impact being felt most severely by the least skilled occupations. (JHR)

103. Donelly, William A.; Havenner, Arthur M.; Hong, B. D.; Hopkins, Frank E.; and Morlan, Terry H. Estimating a Comprehensive County-Level Forecasting Model of the United States - READ. Washington, D.C.: Federal Energy Administration, Revised, August 1977. Mimeographed.

The Regional Energy Activity and Demographic (READ) Model addresses questions concerning the state and local effects of shifts in the demand for energy in response to exogenous shocks (oil embargos, change in oil prices) and to national energy policy decisions. It is divided into four sections: 1) industrial location, 2) construction activity, 3) population, employment and income, and 4) state and local government activity. The model uses eleven years of annual data from 1965 to 1975 and forecasts through 1990. All four sectors are integrated with the Structural Econometric Energy Demand (SEED) model. Estimates are carried using county level data, but forecasts and simulations can be presented at regional levels. In relation to the third section, population and labor force forecasts are presented by age, sex, and race in relation to economic, demographic and energy variables. The employment and wages analysis is undertaken using the model industrial classification breakdown.

104. Earley, Ronald F.; Mohtadi, Malek M.; Rossidivito, Eugene L.; Serot, David E.; and Weisman, Harold. Macroeconomic and Sector Implications of Installing 2.2 Million Residential Solar Units. Washington, D.C.: U.S. Department of Energy, Energy Information Administration, April 1979. DOE/EIA-0102/51

This study analyzes both the sector output (employment) and macro-economic effects of a residential solar installation program of 2.2 million solar units cumulatively installed from 1976-1985. Two systems are considered: 1) solar hot water and 2) solar heating and hot water with liquid as a heat transfer mechanism. The Data Resources Inc. (DRI) macroeconomic forecasting model and the Energy Disaggregated Input-Output (EDIO) model are used. A number of factors increased GNP in the macroeconomic results. Of interest is the result that the new income earned in the design, production and installation of systems is spent, which results in an increase in real output and employment in the economy. The change in the level of GNP is not large, but shifts in the final demand effect the composition of employment. The expansion of $1 billion in the 1985 real GNP, due to the solar scenario, resulted in an increase in the real gross output of $2 billion. This output leads to an increase in net employment of 58.8 thousand jobs. This is a one-tenth of a percent increase. The impact on employment in major sectors is also given.

105. Earley, Ronald F. and Mohtadi, Malek M. Sector Employment Implications of Alternative Energy Scenarios. Washington, D.C.: U.S. Department of Energy, August 21, 1978. DOE/EIA-0102/17

The memorandum uses five energy scenarios reflecting assumptions about economic growth and energy supply. It examines their implications in terms of the structure of employment in the U.S. economy for year 1985. It is divided into three sections. The first part explains the model and simulation procedures. The employment analysis is performed with an input-output (I/O) model which projects employment for 1985 on a job basis for 129 sectors of the economy. The second section discusses the relationship between the changes in the level and composition of final demand and employment. It is based on jobs required to produce $1 billion of sales of each of the final demand components used in the simulation procedure. A $1 billion expenditure for final demand generates, in general, fewer jobs in agriculture, mining and construction, than in manufacturing, distribution and services. The third section discusses the employment implications of the five energy scenarios. Changes in employment requirements are related to the underlying changes in final demand components. Two separate approaches are used. The first approach combines energy forecasts from Projet Independence Evaluation System (PIES) for each of the energy scenarios with the Data Resource, Inc. (DRI) macroeconomic forecast used to define energy scenario. The second approach combines energy forecast from PIES for each of the energy scenario with DRI trendlong macroeconomic forecast. Projected employment levels associated with high demand/high supply (A) and high demand/low supply (B) exceed employment with medium range (C) by 1.3 million jobs. Both low demand/high supply (D) and low demand/low supply (E) have lower levels of employment relative to the medium range (2.5 million and 2.8 million, respectively). The second approach show that the employment impacts of scenarios A and E relative to C are small in comparison with B and D. The sector distribution of the impacts is uniform. The service and distribution sectors are the most impacted followed by the manufacturing sector.

106. Eckstein, Albert J. and Heien, Dale M. A Review of Energy Models with Particular Reference to Employment and Manpower Analysis. Washington, D.C.: Department of Labor, Employment and Training Administration, March 1978.

The study recognizes the interdependence between the general economy and the energy sector. The application of quantitative models to energy-employment issues is tackled by decomposing the energy problem into three phases. The post-embargo shock effects had led to higher prices and more uncertainty. The negative employment impact was clear. The intermediate process of adjustment relates to the substitution phenomenon undertaken by firms and individuals. New employment patterns result from these new production and consumption patterns. The long-run equilibrium phase is the most important in terms of manpower policy by emphasizing the new mix of skills associated with the new employment patterns. With this setting, the study reviews the existing energy models in terms of addressing the employment problems of these three phases.

Models are classified into three types. The first type examines the interdependence between energy industries and the aggregate economy. The second type focuses on the energy industries per se. The third type represents energy sub-sector models. In general, the models have not directly focused on employment and manpower aspects of energy. The main employment adjustments are to take place during the intermediate phase. The long-run equilibrium labor demand of increased energy output is not expected to be large. The study further examines the appropriateness, usefulness and adaptability of particular models to the determination of employment effects. Finally, energy employment and manpower research issues are discussed in relation to substitution, balance of payments, investment and new construction, economic growth and inflation as well as the distribution of income.

107. Farzin, Yeganeh Hossein. The Effect of Discount Rate and Substitute Technology on Depletion of Exhaustible Resources. Washington, D.C.: The World Bank, 1982. Staff Working Paper No. 516.

This paper analyses the validity of several well established propositions in the theory of exhaustible resources in the presence of substitutes. By carefully modelling the technologies of resources extraction and substitute production, we show that:

(a) Despite its widespread acceptance in the literature, the basic proposition that a reduction (an increase) in the rate of discount leads to greater conservation (faster depletion) of an exhaustible resource is not generally valid. It is shown that the effect of a change in the discount rate on the rate of resource depletion depends on capital requirements for development and production of the substitute, capital requirements in resource extraction and the size of the resource stock.

(b) When there are decreasing returns in production of the substitute, the conventional proposition that a relatively high-cost substitute should not be utilized before the stock of the resource is exhausted is invalid. It is shown that in such cases the optimality requires that both the resource and substitute be produced simultaneously for some period of time.

(c) When substitute technology shows increasing returns to scale, the conventional proposition that the marginal cost of the substitute provides a ceiling for the price of the exhaustible resource does not hold. We show that, under such conditions there will be a time interval during which the price of the resource exceeds the marginal cost of the substitute and yet the substitute ought not to be introduced during the interval.

(d) When there are a number of substitutes for the resource, each having a different marginal production cost and a different fixed cost associated with its development and introduction, the conventional rule that "the substitute with the lowest marginal cost of production should be introduced first" is not generally valid. We derive a more general decision rule which requires one to develop and introduce the substitute which yields the largest flow of net social benefit per time period regardless of its effect on the value of the resource stock. (WB)

108. Ferris, Gregg and Mason, Bert. A Review of Regional Economic Models with Special Reference to Labor Impact Assessment. Golden, Colorado: Solar Energy Research Institute, June 1979. SERI/TR-53-100

The study undertakes to develop methods to assess the regional employment implications of solar energy commercialization. Different regional economic models are evaluated. The idea is to prove that solar energy is more labor intensive than conventional energy industries with a positive impact on the labor market. Five models are reviewed: economic base analysis, demographic-economic interaction models, shift-share analysis, input-output analysis, and industrial location analysis. Ten regional models are reviewed along some sought criteria. No one model meets all the criteria. Therefore, more than one model needs to be selected. Final selection requires flexibility or ability to make model modifications.

109. Gallagher, J. Michael; Barany, Ronald; Paskerk, Paul F.; and Zimmerman, Ralph G. J. Resource Requirements, Impacts, and Potential Constraints Associated with Various Energy Futures. Annual report prepared by Bechtel Corporation, Washington, D.C.: U.S. Energy Research and Development Administration, March 1977. APAE-11735-77-1 (NTIS)

This is the first annual report describing an effort by Bechtel Corporation to adapt and apply the Energy Supply Planning Model (ESPM) to the support of the systems analysis activities of the United States Energy Research and Development Administration. Office of the Assistant Administrator for Planning Analysis and Evaluation (ERDA/APAE). The primary emphasis of this program is the identification of resource requirements and the associated impacts and potential constraints associated with various future energy options for this country.

This report summarizes the major activities and accomplishments of the program in fiscal year 1976. Accomplishments include model application and analysis of energy scenarios derived from the 1976 update of the ERDA National Plan and the "1976 National Energy Outlook" of the Federal Energy Administration; analysis of the availability of engineers, manual manpower, and selected materials and equipment commodities; addition of aluminum, carbon steel, and allow steel materials requirements to the model data base; the addition of several kinds of energy facilities to the modeling system; and refinement of the various aspects of the model and data base.

What has emerged from this program and other studies is the need for a clear statement of the nation's energy policy that, in turn, will encourage the orderly expansion of industrial capacity and the availability of adequate supplies of capital, labor, and material resources needed to meet future energy needs. In addition, a comprehensive information system and data base is needed to anticipate resource requirements and monitor the availability of the required resources. (BC)

110. Gallagher, J. Michael and Zimmerman, Ralph G.J. Regional
Requirements of Capital, Manpower, Materials and Equipment for Selected
Energy Futures. Report prepared by Bechtel Corporation. Washington,
D.C.: U.S. Energy Research and Development Administration, November
1976. APAE-11735-76-5

Implementation of national energy policy decisions concerning
development of new energy sources or expansion of old sources will
inevitably result in differential regional impacts. This report
describes the first analysis carried out by Bechtel for the U.S.
Energy Research and Development Administration (ERDA) on the subject
of the regional resource requirements associated with future energy
development strategies. The regional distribution of resource
impacts has been calculated using the Energy Supply Planning Model
developed by Bechtel for the National Science Foundation and ERDA.

Requirements of capital, manpower, materials, equipment, land, and
water are derived for the direct construction and operation of
energy-related facilities. These requirements have been derived
for four cases centering on the Reference Case ($13 price of
imported oil) from the FEA "1976 National Energy Outlook." Three
sensitivity cases tested the impacts of:

    o A synthetic fuels program
    o Continued price regulation of domestic oil and gas
    o Restrictions on coal and nuclear fuel development, as well
       as the above price regulations

Results of the analysis indicate that ten-year (1976-85) cumulative
construction capital costs (in constant 1974 dollars, excluding
owner's costs) are $507 billion for the reference case. These
costs increase by $9 billion with a synthetic fuels program and
decrease by $67 billion for the case with price regulations and
other restrictions on energy development. (BC)

111. Hahn, William F. "Construction Manpower Demand Systems,"
Proceedings of the First Auber Energy Workshop - Socioeconomic Impact of
Electrical Energy Construction, Snowbird, Utah, August 22-26, 1977.
Sponsored by the Tennessee Valley Authority, 1977, pp. 175-192.

Construction Manpower Demand System (CMDS) is a comprehensive
information system that is designed to provide current construction
data and to forecast future volume, composition, geographic distribution and associated labor requirements of construction activity
at the regional and local levels. Manpower demand is a function of
estimated future construction activity. It involves the development of activity projections in dollars and their conversion into
labor requirements by craft. Among the potential users are the
Department of Labor (DOL), the Department of Energy (DOE), and the
Tennessee valley Authority (TVA). TVA is a major producer of
electric power and a major constructor of generation facilities.
CMDS would identify craft bottlenecks. Skill shortages affect
ultimately consumer rates given that construction labor accounts
for about 30 percent of total cast of a nuclear generating station.
It would also assist TVA in its social and economic impact assessment. DOL is responsible for the overall CMDS effort. TVA's

responsibility is to monitor and estimate labor requirements of energy-related construction and will operate the energy subsector of the system.

112. Hannon, Bruce. "An Energy Standard of Value," The Annals of the American Economy, Vol. 410, November 1973, pp. 139-153.

An energy research group at the University of Illinois Center for Advanced Computation (CAC) is investigating the use of energy in the United States. The CAC model provides for the total energy cost of goods and services, the use of energy by type, employment by occupation and pollution for 362 sectors representing the industrial and commercial economy. Three areas for energy conservation are discussed. 1) Production efficiency: employers do not strive to use energy efficiently and industries have become more energy-intensive and less labor-intensive. If economic growth is desired, the impact on energy use should be minimized and employment demands maximized. 2) Product use efficiency: the variety of goods and services available provides overchoice. Certain products are more energy efficient per unit of service than others. If the nation were to shift to such products, there will be saving of energy and a rise in employment. 3) The rate of energy use needs to be restricted based on knowledge of the family dependence on total energy for housing, clothing, food and transportation. Achieving energy conservation can be done through 1) education or socialization programs that present energy cost of alternatives goods and services to consumers and 2) governmental regulations of energy use (rationing and incentive schemes) and control of high energy consumption practices.

113. Hannon, Bruce; Stein, Richard G.; Segal B.Z.; and Serber, Diane. "Energy and Labor in the Construction Sector," Science, Vol. 202, November 24, 1978, pp. 837-847.

This study utilizes an energy input-output model to investigate energy and employment in the construction industry. The model determines the impact of construction activities on total national energy consumption in 1967 and studies the patterns of total energy use and employment within various construction categories. It shows that for the construction of new buildings, total energy consumption could be reduced by 20 percent. This could be accomplished by selecting less energy-intensive building materials and assemblies for fixed programmatic requirements, by expending energy in construction to minimize the total lifetime energy costs of buildings, and by energy conservation in industries that supply direct and indirect inputs to the construction sector of the economy. The authors suggest that the government could expand its energy conservation programs in the construction sector and outlines an appropriate and effective policy.

114. Hoffman, Lutz. "Energy Demand and Its Determinants in Brazil," TIMS Studies in the Management Sciences, 17, 1981, pp. 361-394.

This paper provides a detailed description of Brazil's energy demand since 1955. For the year 1970 the end use of energy is broken down into commercial and non-commercial energy as well as industrial activities. Whereas the structure of Brazil's commercial energy consumption is comparable to that of other large developing countries, the data for non-commercial energy use reveal the surprising fact that 25 percent of Brazil's non-commercial energy is consumed in the manufacturing sector. This is quite different from what has been found (or assumed) for other developing countries.

The change of energy demand over time is first analyzed by a shift approach which shows that the growth effect dominates, followed by the structural effect, and then a very small intensity effect. In an econometric time series analysis Brazil's long-run income elasticity of energy demand is estimated at 1.25 and the long-run price elasticity at -0.27. If the impact of structural change is eliminated the income elasticity comes down to 0.94.

In an analysis of energy demand in the industrial sector demand functions derived from production functions are estimated for various industries. It is found that neither a Cobb-Douglas type of demand function nor a translogarithmic version produce satisfactory results. However, very good results are obtained with a dual of Cobb-Douglas type demand function. The results are interesting with respect to the specification of the demand function and the estimated parameters. They basically confirm the hypothesis of energy-capital complementarity and energy-labour substitutability. (NHP)

115. Holcombe, Randall G. The Economic Impact of An Interruption in the United States Petroleum Imports: 1975-2000. Washington, D.C.: Department of the Navy, Office of Naval Research, November 1974.

The objective of this study is to estimate the economic impact of a possible interruption in petroleum imports during the period 1975-2000 by using an input-output model of the U.S. economy. This effort is believed to be an integral part of any rational energy policy. The model disaggregates the economy into 82 sectors and the evaluation is carried on both sectoral and aggregate bases. The effects of both supply and demand constraints are included in the model. The study projects oil consumption up to year 2000 and its share of total energy consumption. Different scenarios (high and low import estimates) are used to project petroleum imports. The vulnerability of the U.S. economy to any interruption in imports tends to increase in the future. Examining the future sources of U.S. petroleum imports reveals increasing reliance on the Middle East. It is estimated that the cost of a total embargo of imports from the Middle East for a year would be in the range of $49 and $117 billion. Its impact on the economy is significant. The high estimate of a 7.2 percent reduction in GNP would cause a severe recession and a double-digit unemployment.

116. Kramer Associates, Inc. A Plan for Developing a Comprehensive Energy Manpower Information System. Washington, D.C.: U.S. Department of Energy, Office of Education, Business and Labor Affairs, September 1979. DOE/IR-10233 UC-2, 13 (NTIS)

This report focuses on the manpower and employment dimensions of energy alternatives. It provides the analytical framework for assessing energy manpower supply and demand. Energy production by source and technology is related to employment by industry, occupation, location, and education and training requirements. It accounts for labor mobility and attrition. It describes a plan for a Comprehensive Energy Manpower Information System (CEMIS). It documents the baseline and answers questions implicit in energy program changes or the impact of energy program changes or the reduction and source shifts on the employment levels. Energy manpower data availability appears adequate for coal and petroleum with some revisions. For the nuclear generation of electricity more statistical series are needed. For solar and geothermal energy data series are nonexistent and definitional clarity is needed. It is recommended that DOE establishes an organizational unit in charge of CEMIS to remedy present data deficiencies and to institute new data.

117. Mukherjee, Shiskir K. "Energy Policy and Planning in India," Energy, 6, August 1981, pp. 823-51.

The energy crisis has imposed increasing economic strains on India and is interfering with its industrialization and development efforts. The energy resources and energy consumption patterns are reviewed in this paper. It also evaluates the major energy policy recommendations and energy forecasts of the working group on Energy Policy (WEP) which was formed in 1977 to assess the energy situation in India and to develop a perspective for the end of the century. The paper points out the need for a comprehensive analysis of energy policy within the context of a national energy-economic modelling framework. A broad framework is presented and consists of four interlinked models: a macroeconomic model, a demand forecasting model, an energy supply model and an economic impact model. The purpose of this integrated model would be to tie the needs of the energy sector with the rest of the economy. Alternative economic scenarios lead to different energy demand forecasts. The supply models based on these forecasts will provide data for investment needs and energy prices to be fed back into the demand models for a modified set of demand forecasts. The economic impact model would provide manpower and material requirements for the energy sector for a given supply scenario. The consistency of such investment requirements within the overall macro-economic framework could be seen from the macro-economic model.

118. Petersen, H. Craig. Sector-Specific Output and Employment Impacts of a Solar Space and Water Heating Industry. Washington, D.C.: National Science Foundation, December, 1977.

There is little available information on sector-specific sales and employment impacts of a large-scale solar space and water heating industry. This study identifies those sectors of the economy which would be most affected by increased solar utilization and estimates the magnitude of the changes.

The basic methodology involves augmenting an existing Input/Output table to include sectors reflecting solar technology. Data

required to augment the matrix were obtained from questionnaires
returned by existing firms involved in collector manufacture or
solar space and water heating system sales.   The augmented I/O
matrix was inverted to generate a direct and indirect requirements
matrix.   The elements of this matrix estimate the changes in total
sector output resulting from changes in final demand of other
sectors.   Estimates of final demand for solar heating systems by
1985 and projections of energy savings associated with solar
installations to that time were obtained from existing studies.
Using the computed direct and indirect requirements matrix and the
assumed changes in the composition of final demand, estimates of
changes in sales and employment were derived for 131 sectors of the
U.S. economy.

It was determined that the sectors most affected by solar development will be those involved in electricity generation and the
mining, refining, and fabrication of metals, especially copper.
The proportionate changes in industry sales and employment are not
expected to be very great.   Only copper rolling and drawing is
changed by as much as 2 percent.   This finding suggests that the
government can proceed with programs designed to accelerate solar
space and water heating usage without fear of adversely affecting
any sector of the economy or creating excessive demands for natural
resources or productive capacity.   (NSF)

119. Samouilidis, J.E. and Mitropoulos, C. S.   "Energy and Economic
Growth in Industrializing Countries: The Case of Greece," Energy
Economics, Vol. 6, No. 3, July, 1984, pp. 191-201.

This paper uses numerous econometric models to investigate aspects
of the interrelated paths of economic growth and energy demand in
the Greek economy.   Some of the studies presented argue that the
basic mechanism through which energy affects are reflected is the
interrelationship between energy, capital and labor.   These three
inputs experience substitutability to a limited extent.   There
tends to be a bias toward labor-energy substitutes due to elementary production technologies.   However, on the aggregate level
substitution is restricted.   The findings in this article explain
and emphasize the difficulty of manpower planning in the energy
sector.

120. Seltzer, N. and Schriver, William R.   "Forecasting Manpower
Requirements for Nuclear Power Plant Construction," Proceedings of the
International Atomic Energy Agency, Vienna, Austria, 1978, pp. 391-406.
IAEA-SM 223/20

This paper presents the estimates of labor requirements for the
construction of nuclear fueled electricity generating plants.   It
examines the methodology and results of a segment of the overall
Construction Manpower Demand System (CMDS) covering 1977-1981.
Plants were classified by geographic region, type and size.   Ten
geographic locations and 29 construction crafts are used as the
basis of the forecasting.   A residual cost approach is used to
determine total labor required in the past and to calculate the
percentage changes in the scope of work.   It is then extrapolated
by applying it to the man-months per megawatt or kilowatt values.

The results indicate a 20 percent increases in man-hours required per kilowatt of capacity. Forecasts by a national basis show that labor demand will increase from 65,700 work-years in 1977 to an estimated 96,594 work-years in 1981. The national projections data for 1977-81 are presented on a monthly and by craft basis.

121. Stenehjem, E.J. Summary Description of Seam: The Social and Economic Assessment Model. Argonne, Illinois: Argonne National Laboratory, April 1978.

The Social Economic Assessment Model (SEAM) is the descriptive name of a series of submodels and data bases that have been integrated and computerized. These components were developed as a natural consequence of long involvement in the prediction and assessment of social, economic and institutional changes accompanying energy development. The data and models of SEAM can be used dependently or interactively for any county or combination of counties in the United States. The model is the Impact Project Model which forecasts (1) annual direct employment requirements for most forms of energy extraction and conversion facilities; and (2) annual estimates of indirect (secondary) employment requirements created by the presence of the new energy or industrial facility. By specifying the new energy or industrial project to be evaluated, the year in which the facility construction begins and the name of the county or counties where it will be located, the user can determine the annual construction and operations work force requirements for the life of the facility. Using an employment multiplier derived from the export base theory, the secondary employment requirements can also be determined.

122. Stenehjem, E.J. and Metzger, J. E. A Framework for Projecting Employment and Population Changes Accompanying Energy Development, Phase I. Argonne, Illinois: Argonne National Laboratory, Energy and Environmental Systems Division, May 1980.

This study provides an information system that can be used to forecast county employment and population changes that are associated with the construction and operation of eight different energy technologies. The technologies are limited to those that were expected to be used in the mid-1980s. These technologies are: coal extraction, oil-shale extraction and conversion, offshore oil and gas extraction, nuclear power plants, liquification plants and geothermal facilities. The direct employment requirements, as well as the secondary or support positions created by energy development are projected. The data reveals that a strong generic relationship exists between the employment requirements of the energy industry and the population growth of the county. Other energy planning factors that can be estimated to include the proportion of secondary positions that are made available in each annual period and the number of residents available in the county to fill the positions.

123. Stenehjem, J. and Metzger, J. E. A Framework for Projecting Employment and Population Changes Accompanying Energy Development: Phase II. Argonne, Illinois: Argonne National Laboratory, May 1980.

This study describes several spatial assignment models for the allocation of in-migrants and their service needs to energy-impacted communities. Two demand-oriented models (gravity and linear programming) are evaluated. The spatial allocation model (SAM) that incorporates both supply and demand characteristics of the location decision is also discussed. The public services and facility requirements are categorized by type (urban, rural) and size of communities. They cover: water and sewage, solid waste management, education, health care, recreation, police and fire, library, social welfare and general government. Several tables are developed to quantitatively describe the standards for manpower and facilities necessary in the provision of services by local government. This is followed by an explanation of the procedures for determining local service and facility requirements. Several factors need to be kept in mind to determine appropriate standards for differing communities. Examples include regional and/or site variations, socio-economic characteristics, state legislation and the like. Finally, the technical specifications of the spatial assignment models are described in the appendix.

124. "Studying Energy Employment Relations," Solar Heating and Cooling, Vol. 5, No. 3, March 1980, pp. 24-25.

Employment will remain an uncertain criterion for determining energy policy until a more suitable economic model is developed to accommodate many unpredictable variables. To determine the employment potential of solar energy, it is important to figure out the relative cost of solar energy to conventional fuels. If solar turns to have a cost advantage, a net gain of 2.9 million jobs could be achieved by 1990 when resources are committed to it.

125. United Nations Association of the United States of America. Economic Policy Council. Energy and Employment: Issues and Agenda for Research. New York: United Nations, June 1979.

The energy-employment interactions are defined in terms of a) the overall economic issues, b) the industrial, occupational, and regional issues, and c) the international issues. The study reviews what research work has been completed or under way on energy-job issues. After contacting all the appropriate agencies (universities, research institutions and government agencies) it appears that very few studies were undertaken dealing with specific employment impacts. Upon reviewing the state of the art, several models were developed. They help estimate the relative effects of alternative policies. But, the results of outputs must be evaluated in the light of the underlying assumptions. In the U.S., it appears that not much weight is assigned to job implications of current energy programs or of alternative energy strategies. Only piecemeal efforts and scattered studies that lack coordination or high priority exist. The problem seems to be one of the lack of analytical tools and poor data base. Research on energy-jobs relationships should be given high priority. The following areas have been specified: 1) The substitution or complementarity of capital, labor and energy. 2) The impact of changing energy supply and price on geographic and industrial shifts in demand,

production, and employment. 3) The employment effects of conservation and of altering the energy-mix. It is extremely important to
focus on the job aspects of energy self-sufficiency. Finally,
intensive consideration should be given to relocation and retraining programs.

126. U.S. Department of Energy. Joint Egypt United States Report on
Egypt/ United States Cooperative Energy Assessment, Volume 5, Annex 13.
Washington, D.C.: U.S. Department of Energy, April 1979.
DOE/IA-0002105

Implementation of national energy policy decisions concerning
development of new energy sources or expansion of old sources will
inevitably result in significant requirements for a nation's
resources of capital, labor, materials and equipment. This report
on the implementation requirements of alternative Egyptian energy
futures describes the first analysis carried out by Bechtel for the
International Energy Development Program of the U.S. Department of
Energy.

The analysis is based on Bechtel's Energy Supply Planning Model
(ESPM), which provides a systematic means of calculating, based on
any user-specified energy development strategy, the total resources
required directly to build and operate the energy supply facilities
needed to implement the strategy. The ESPM was developed originally for the analysis of energy options in the United States, and
the model has seen extensive use in supporting the analysis of U.S.
energy plans. The energy assessment of Egypt marks its first use
by Bechtel in analyzing energy options outside the United States.
Accordingly, a major task in the current study was to develop a
methodology to adapt the model and data base to conditions appropriate to the Egyptian energy system. The adaptation methodology
involved conversion of existing ESPM estimates from a U.S. basis to
an Egyptian basis using factors for Egyptian wage rates, labor
project efficiency, expatriate labor usage, import surcharges on
capital goods, and other variables. In addition, facility sizes
were scaled downward when appropriate. It was recognized that a
thorough conversion effort would not be possible given the study's
limited time and budget; however, it was believed that even the
limited effort could provide useful internally-consistent
"ballpark" estimates of resource requirements.

The adapted model and data base was applied to a comparison case
energy development program as specified by the DOE, as well as
several alternative cases testing the sensitivity of resource
requirements to lower levels of nuclear power, increased use of
natural gas or renewable energy resources, and improved efficiency
of energy use. Cumulative capital costs of the comparison case
amount to roughly ₤E 18 billion, in constant January 1978 Egyptian
pounds, exclusive of land costs, interest during construction, or
escalation. Roughly 75 percent of these requirements accrue to the
electric utility sector. Construction labor requirements increase
from 5,800 man-years in 1976 to 50,000 man-years in 2000, whereas
the operations and maintenance requirements increase from 5,800
man-years to 32,000 man-years over the period. The assumptions on
the use of foreign labor and material lead to results that the

import component represents about 80 percent of total capital
costs, about 20 percent of operating costs, and about 25 percent of
construction labor requirements. Cumulative capital costs are
reduced by up to 15 percent over the range of sensitivity cases
evaluated. A particularly significant finding of the sensitivity
analysis was the postulated oil production levels are not sufficient to allow oil to continue to substitute its position from oil
exporter to oil importer. (DOE)

127. U.S. Department of Energy. Manpower for Energy Research: A
Comprehensive Manpower Information System for Energy Research,
Development and Demonstration. Washington, D.C.: U.S. Department of
Energy, February 1978. HCP/U6046-01 (NTIS)

This report focuses on the development of a comprehensive manpower
information system for energy research and development. The system
should take advantage of existing data sources and ensure standard-
ization of definitions, improved sampling, and the like among all
reporting bodies. DOE should establish a staff whose responsibility is to develop and utilize the system on an on-going basis.
It is recommended that the issue of complete computerization be
reviewed by a panel of manpower experts. It is further recommended
that an interagency committee on energy manpower information be
established to link the efforts of other government agencies with
the DOE. The report focuses on the development of manpower information for energy RD& D manpower and accordingly presents specific
recommendations to that effect. A base line measure needs to be
established to provide a comprehensive measure of scientific and
technical personnel (STP) engaged in energy RD&D by field of energy
and selected occupations covering both private and public funded
research and development. Also, it is important to have a directory of establishments conducting energy RD&D, and to institute a
system of periodic reporting as well as a reporting system on DOE
training support. Other improvements cover employment, labor
market and mobility, earnings, education and training data.

128. U.S. Department of Labor and U.S. Department of Energy.
Projections of Cost on On-Site Manual Labor Requirements for
Constructing Electric Generating Plants, 1980-1990. Washington D.C.:
DOE, February 1982. DOE/ER-0130 (NTIS)

The objective of the study is to provide estimates on capital costs
and labor requirements for power plant construction to be used by
all interested organizations. On-site labor requirements are
estimated for 14 craft classifications and 10 geographic areas.
The study first tackles the electric generating capacity additions
and associated labor requirements. The unit capital costs and
labor requirements for nominal facilities are given. This is
followed by a presentation of the national and regional labor
requirements.

The appendices outline the forecasting models, the electric power
plant projects, the estimation of construction labor requirements,
and cost functions as well as the regional and national electric
capacity additions. Major findings reveal 1) regional shifts in
construction, 2) a general decline of activity between 1980-1990,

3) a change of emphasis in the major construction trades, and 4) increase in real costs of construction of new generating capacity. Towards the second half of the eighties, labor requirements are projected to increase after experiencing a significant decrease in the early eighties.

4
Socio-economic Impacts
of Energy Production

129. Al-Essa, Johayna S. "The Influence of the Oil Industry on Labor Modernization: A Field Study," Journal of Gulf and Arab Peninsula Studies, Vol. 6, No. 22, April 53-70. (in Arabic)

The study investigates the role of a factory (petroleum enterprise) and its effects on modernizing the individual and his beliefs and values. It assumes the petroleum enterprise to be a modernizing school as the individuals associated with an industrial environment are more receptive to modern trends than others. A field study was undertaken in Qatar. A questionnaire was developed and distributed to two samples. The first sample included 73 workers from Shell and Qatar Oil Companies. The second sample was made up of 50 individuals not associated with the oil industry. The topics under investigation were diverse and included: effective participation, motivation, ambitions, consumption patterns, efficiency, size of family, general knowledge, family responsibilities, new skills, women's rights, and channels of communication, etc. The findings reveal that the industrial activities in Qatar did not modernize the individual. This is attributed to the lack of supportive contributing forces as education, urbanization, communications and the like.

130. Arab Labor Organization. Oil and Petrochemical Labor Office. Social Services System for Petroleum and Chemical Workers in Iraq Compared with Other Arab Oil Countries. Baghdad, Iraq: ALO, 1979. (in Arabic)

This work is one of seven studies that tackles the legislative, technical, training-related, organizational and vocational aspects of workers in the oil and chemical sector. There are wide differences in the system of social services among countries. It is reflective of the socio-economic background of the country in question. The study identifies the basic indicators in support of a social security system as it evolved in the literature and evaluates accordingly the corresponding system for oil and chemical workers in the Arab countries.

131. Aviel, David S. The Politics of Nuclear Energy. Washington, D.C.: University of America Press, 1982.

The book surveys the attitudes of 142 senators, congressman and Governors regarding the issue of nuclear energy. The Three Mile Island accident events are evaluated including the decontamination and cleanup as well as the communications problem. The attitudes are assessed along several dimensions. In relation to the ranking of energy sources, coal and more oil exploration ranked high among respondents. Solar energy followed and nuclear energy came fourth. The safety record was perceived adequate by half of the group. The majority felt, however, that there is a need to tighten government regulation of the nuclear industry in order to increase safety. It was also felt that appropriations for nuclear research and development should be increased. There was predominant agreement against federal government ownership. The study also presents the difference of opinions between Republics and Democrats.

132. Baker, Joe G. Determinants of Coal Mine Labor Productivity Change-A Progress Report. Oak Ridge Tennessee: ORAU, January 1979.

This monograph focuses on the labor productivity decline in bituminous coal and lignite mining and its implications on labor demand, working conditions and costs of production. The research study uses different analytical approaches and different data sets. The Illinois data and the Bureau of Mines data compiled at the state and national levels are used. Four hypotheses were tested to unveil the causes of such productivity drop: 1) resource base, 2) technological aspects of the production process, 3) changes in the institutional set-up, and 4) changes pertinent to the coal mine work force. The decline is attributed to the Coal Mine Health and Safety Act (CMHSA) of 1969. Surface mining productivity decline appears to be related to state reclamation legislation and changes in mine size.

133. Baron, C. "Energy Policy and Social Progress in Developing Countries," International Labour Review, Vol. 119, September/October, 1980, pp. 531-548.

This article reviews the implications of energy scarcity as a result of the second oil shock, for the developing countries in terms of employment generation and the alleviation of poverty. The orthodox solution to the problem posed by higher oil prices now facing developing countries is to increase the domestic production of primary energy in order to reduce level of oil imports required. The costs of modern energy technologies are very high. The labor force in the energy sector - with the exception of coal mining - is highly skilled but small in relation to output. The construction of hydroelectric, geothermal and nuclear plants tends to be capital- intensive. Conservation policy presents an alternative that results in economies in the requirements of the energy sector for capital and foreign exchange and higher growth rates of output and employment. In the U.S., the additional employment generated as a consequence of energy conservation was analyzed. A conservation policy would create millions of jobs in the manufacture and installation of insulation equipment and small scale energy devices. Moreover, to achieve the satisfaction of basic needs, it is imperative to improve the supply and use of energy at the level of the village itself. Yet, the implementation

of renewable technologies poses formidable technical, economic and
institutional constraints. The role of the ILO in relation to
energy transition includes training activities to promote energy
conservation, the application of more efficient primary energy
recovery and conversion techniques and the application of small-
scale renewable energy technologies. One important conclusion
raised is that more research is needed in energy use and its
relationship to growth of output and employment.

134. Commoner, B. "Energy and Labor: Job Implications of Energy
Development or Shortage," Alternatives, Summer 1978, pp. 4-13.

The Canadian economy confronts three serious and simultaneous
problems: unemployment, environment and energy. It is maintained
that there is a trade-off between them. These problems cannot be
solved all at once, there must be sacrifice. If that's the case,
the author would favor actions to reduce unemployment at the
expense of environmental consequences and energy use. The solution
of the unemployment problem is at the heart of the improvement of
human welfare. But, the author argues that the crisis in employment, energy, and the environment represents the same crisis. The
article shows how the production and use of energy, the labor
requirements, and the impact on the environment interrelate.
Unemployment is part of the same economic trends that generated
both the energy crisis and the environmental problems. The argu-
ments presented tackle the use of non-renewable energy sources with
escalating prices, the availability of capital and the rate of new
investment, the impact of different forms of energy on labor demand
and on working conditions. The National Energy Plan of the Carter
Administration is evaluated within this framework. It is expected
to worsen, not alleviate, the energy crisis, with negative effects
on the interrelated issues of inflation, unemployment and the
economy. The alternative offered is that of solar energy. Such
programs would stabilize the price of energy, slow down inflation,
generate jobs and solve the energy crisis. The case of solar
energy is discussed. An independent labor position on energy could
provide a powerful remedy to the serious economic problems under
discussion.

135. Critchlow, Robert V. "Technology and Labor in Electric Power and
Gas Industry," Monthly Labor Review, Volume 101, Number 11, Nov. 1978,
pp. 19-22.

The article addresses the impact of technological developments on
employment, occupations and labor requirements. First, the widespread use of computers in new and old generating plants in
different operations creates a demand for people in computer-
related occupations (system analysts, programmers and peripheral
equipment operators). The need for keypunch operators will decline
with the use of display terminals. Second, as nuclear generation
of electric power becomes more important and to reach an estimated
18.6 percent of total generating capacity by 1985, there will be a

clear need for more highly trained workforces. Construction and maintenance work in nuclear plants requires higher skills for some crafts (e.g. welders). Also, nuclear plants require relatively more scientists, engineers, and technicians than other types of generating plants. Third, coal for fuel technology has higher labor requirements than those of oil-fired or natural gas fired one. Fourth, the vehicles used in construction and maintenance of transmission and distribution lines have experienced considerable technological changes. The mobile equipment are more mechanized and require smaller crews. But the growing size of the mobile fleet requires more labor resources. The utility industry has launched well-developed training programs to bridge the gap for the different technological advancements.

136. Cruze, Alejandro. "Latin American Energy Corporation and Its Projection to Other Developing Countries." Paper presented at the Third Arab Energy Conference–Energy and Cooperation, Algiers, May 4-9, 1985. Safat, Kuwait: OAPEC, 1985.

Energy cooperation in Latin America has taken place within the Latin American integration process. This has resulted in bilateral and multilateral movements through specific energy development projects. This process received a strong boost in 1973 when the Latin American Energy Organization (OLADE) was created by the Latin American Energy Cooperation Program (PLACE). PLACE has three objectives: 1) To obtain greater knowledge about national energy resources, particularly hydroenergy, biomass, geothermal and coal potentials. 2) To prepare planning instruments such as method-ologies for energy balances, long-range energy supply and demand analyses and energy information systems. 3) To strengthen the funding mechanisms for cooperation and actions in order to create a Latin American market for energy and technology.

These accomplishments are to promote an effective means of gradually achieving socioeconomic integration in Latin America and cooperating with other Third World regions. Projection will be achieved through exchange of information, strengthening of training centers, development of energy technologies, and specific cooper-ation projects. The paper concludes that the problems and difficulties that exist can only be overcome by pooling technical and human capabilities between Latin America and the Arab World.

137. Drovet, Pierre. "The Restructuring of the Petroleum Refining Sector and Its Social Consequences," International Labor Review, Vol. 123, No. 4, July-August 1984, pp. 423-440.

The oil crises of 1973 and 1979 spurred the reorganization of the petroleum refining sector throughout the world. The result was a considerable reduction in the refinery utilization rate for the industrial countries, and the resurgence of refining activities in the industrializing countries and in the petroleum producing and exporting countries as a whole. The accelerated pace of closures, the contraction of the markets, and the reduction in manpower requirements were also brought about by technological advances, energy-saving efforts, the development of alternative energy sources and the environment protection. The effects on employment generated by the refining industry is less than that of other industries, the indirect employment effects need to be taken into consideration. British trade unions estimate, for example, that in 1983 refineries gave direct employment to 13,000 workers but indirect employment to between 50,000 and 75,000 in allied industries. With regard to industrial relations, trade unions complain from the lack of a well-defined restructuring policy, their limited participation in closure decisions and the lack of concern for social implications. Government, employers and trade unions negotiate remedies covering saving of jobs, preventing layoff and training and retraining.

138. El Zarouk, A. and El Babid, M. K. "The Future of Oil Exploration in the Arab World," Proceedings of the Third Arab Energy Conference, Algiers, May 4-9 1985. Kuwait: OAPEC, 1985. (in Arabic)

Oil exploration slowed down in the late seventies and was restricted to a few countries and in limited quantities. This research work examines the development of such activities over the period 1974-1983 in the Arab countries. The study outlines the different factors responsible for such slowdowns. They cover technical, legislative, manpower (technical and administrative skills) and financial aspects. In conclusion, it is very important to identify the oil reserves in each Arab State not only as a source of energy but also for its importance towards their economic development. Finally, joint Arab effort is imperative in this direction.

139. Farjani, Nader. Immigration to Oil. Beirut, Lebanon: Centre for Arab Unity Studies, 1983. (in Arabic)

The book discusses labor migration to the Arab oil countries and its effects on their socio-economic structure. The migration phenomenon is tackled at both ends: country of origin and destination. The impact of immigration on the national development of the oil-producing countries is thoroughly examined. The movement of labor from the exporting to the importing economies has, through the reallocation of human resources, resulted in widening the socio-economic gap between the two.

140. Federal Emergency Management Agency. Human Needs: Where to get Federal Help during an Energy Emergency. Washington, D.C.: GPO, June 1980.

This publication reviews the types of assistance to be made by Federal Government to meet energy emergencies. Several areas are covered and include housing, food, financial, health and medical help, transportation, federal manpower and equipment, and other services. Programs are individually listed for each area identifying the type of assistance available, its availability, how to get assistance and its limitations.

141. Gilette, Robert. "'Transient' Nuclear Workers: A Special Case for Standards," Science, Vol. 186, October 11, 1974, pp. 125-129.

'Transient' workers constitute a large portion of the nuclear industry's manpower. These workers are guaranteed a half a day's pay for only a few minutes work and help with tasks such as decontaminating equipment and repairing radioactive equipment. The only requirement for these workers is to be at least 18 and be physically able to do the job. Outside employment contractors "recruit" these people and send them to the plant to perform their job for a predetermined amount of minutes to limit radioactive exposure. This article raises concern for these workers and cites examples where they are being exposed to radiation beyond the safe limit and not given proper safety instructions. It is suggested that more clear-cut regulations need to be defined for this area.

142. Granade, Hugh R. "An Approach to Estimating the Number of Movers Attracted to Large Power Construction Projects, "Proceedings of the First Auber Energy Workshop - Socioeconomic Impact of Electrical Energy Construction, Snowbird, Utah, August 22-26, 1977. Sponsored by the Tennessee Valley Authority, 1977, pp. 119-126.

This paper designs a method to estimate the number of construction craftsmen that will move to the site of a large energy construction project. The approach used exhausts first the pool of qualified workers living in the area given the level of manpower demand, the difference is filled by movers from outside the area. The commuting area is defined as a 50-mile radius. Sixteen occupations were considered as specified by the builder. For each development district, the number of workers employed in the base year (1970) is calculated and the number of unemployed workers is added to obtain the total number of workers by category. The target year for a particular craft is taken to be the year where the demand for the craft peaks for a given power project. The rate of growth of the population in the relevant counties is applied to base year total of workers in each occupation to determine the supply of workers by category for the target year. The figures of the different development districts are added. Assuming no wage differential, job applicants will be drawn from the unemployed pool. An estimate of demand by craft is obtained from a manpower demand study by occupation for the development districts in the Tennessee Valley Region over the period 1970-80. The net supply of qualified workers was calculated as the difference between total supply and projected demands (excluding power project demand). The supply covered unionized and non-unionized qualified workers (open shop assumption). If a closed shop assumption is considered, the ratio of unionized workers to total supply of qualified workers needs to be derived and applied to projected total net supply figures. Power project demand forecasts were provided by builder. The difference between demand and net supply figures would determine whether shortages are to be experienced in the target year.

143. Haley, D. Operation Bootstrap: Renewable and Efficient Energy for New York State. Albany, New York: New York State Legislative Commission on Energy Systems, 1977. NP-23796 (NTIS)

Operation Bootstrap is a self-help program designed to make sure that the vast sums spent on energy in New York state are spent to the extent sensible and possible within New York, creating jobs and stimulating business. The theme of the report is how much can be accomplished and how quickly by conservation and renewable energy systems applicable to New York. In Part I, energy independence and conservation are discussed and the following are presented: Efficiency/Conservation in Electricity; Bootstrap Technologies (inertial storage or flywheels, wind energy, bioconversion, solar collectors and cells, new patterns with solar energy, recycling of wastes); Nuclear Energy; Power Transmission; Alternatives to the Electric Distribution System; The Power Authority; The Safe Energy Act; Phantom Taxes in Your Electric Bill; Empire State Power Resources Inc.; Natural Gas; Proposed Gas Rate Surcharge for Gas Exploration; Who Owns What; and The Status Quo. Part II, Jobs and Energy, is an analysis of the employment-creation potential of the Operation Bootstrap approach. (NTIS)

144. Hannon, B. M.; Segal B. Z.; Brodrick, J.; Ford, C.; Joyce, J.; Kakela P.; and Perez-Blanco, H. Energy Conservation and Employment Impacts of Changes in Technology and Consumption. Washington, D.C.: U.S. Energy Research and Development Administration, May 1977.

The potential for energy conservation is examined in relation to several industrial sectors of the economy using an energy/-employment input-output model. Its impacts on energy consumption and employment are assessed for the U.S. The four specific areas studied are: iron and steel, and paper production, electricity-steam cogeneration and residential space conditioning.

145. Hastings, M. and Cawley, M.E. "Community Leaders Perspectives on Socio-Economic Impacts of Power-Plant Development," Energy, Vol. 6, May 1981, pp. 447-456.

The siting and construction of electrical generating facilities have long been of particular concern with regard to their local socioeconomic and environmental impacts. The primary focus of this research effort was to identify and measure the socioeconomic impacts of power plant development on non-metropolitan host communities. A mail survey, distributed to community leaders in 100 power plant communities east of Mississippi River, was utilized to gather information from 713 respondents. Community leaders were asked as to the plant's impact on a) community groups (property owners, elderly people, store owners, farmers and young workers), b) aspects of community life regarding economy, employment and income, public works and transportation, land use and housing, recreation and culture, and public services (crime, schools, medical facilities), c) overall community acceptance and d) attitudes toward power plant development. Four types of plants were examined a) hydroelectric plants b) plants burning, c) nuclear plants, and d) coal burning plants.

Overall the trends and patterns of plant impact on the host communities were found to be largely positive. Specifically, local employment opportunities were generally enhanced with the advent of the power plant. Directly related to power plant development was the overall improvement of the local economic situation - offshoots from such in the economic area included related general improvements in the community quality of life. While the vast majority of community leaders responded with positive comments on power plant presence, adverse impacts were also mentioned. Negative comments focused on environmental problems, deterioration of roads and traffic conditions, and the possibility of nuclear accidents. Despite these negative impacts, almost two-thirds of the community leaders would definitely support the reconstruction of same energy facility. Power plant development, therefore, is generally perceived as both a positive and beneficial asset for the host area. (PPL)

146. Hunter, Ken. "The Basic Question: Are Risks of Nuclear Power Acceptable?" United Mine Workers Journal, June, 1978, pp. 6-8.

The basis of the discussion triggered by this article centers on the expansion of nuclear energy and the associated wastes and risks. Tripling the plants as planned would triple the problems. The nuclear safety debate puzzles the laymen. The disagreement of experts raises serious doubts about the safety of the nuclear industry. It is estimated that the worst case accident in a nuclear power plant yields 145,000 casualties. What are the chances for the worst case to happen? The stand of the insurance industry people could reflect on the answer to the question since they weigh the benefits against the risks. The insurance industry has refused to cover more than a small portion of the risk. The government has reacted to set an arbitrary ceiling of $560 million on liability of nuclear power plants and to totally exempt the manufacturers of nuclear equipment from such liability. It is appropriate to conclude that the risks are not as remote as claimed. Safe and permanent disposal of radioactive nuclear wastes has not been disposed of. New Mexico - having salt domes - refuses to become the nation's nuclear garbage can. California and other states have halted the construction of more nuclear plants until a reliable system of nuclear waste disposal becomes available. In essence, the more you know the more you fear the risks.

147. International Energy Agency. Energy Research Development and Demonstration in the IEA Countries: 1982 Review of National Programmes. Paris: OECD, 1983.

The annual National Energy Research Development and Demonstration Programme Review is undertaken by the Committee on Energy Research and Development (CRD) to support energy technology development towards energy conservation and replacement by native resources in the member countries of the Internal Energy Agency (IEA). Basic information on national policies and organizational structures are described for each country. The appendix presents a review report for each country. The overall report indicates that total budgets for IEA government energy research development and demonstration (RD&D) expenditure for 1982 amounted to $7.174 billion. Budgets have decreased by 9 percent in real terms. It is accounted for by the decrease in the United States budget. Yet there is still commitment to the importance of energy technologies in the structure of future energy systems. Seven energy areas are reviewed:

conservation, oil and gas, coal, conventional nuclear, advanced nuclear, renewable energies, and electrical and other sources. The issue of complementarity of government and industry programmers is an important one. There appears to be a need for a re-evaluation of the appropriate role of international collaborating work including the identification of specific areas and projects.

148. International Energy Agency. Energy Research, Development and Demonstration in the IEA Countries: 1983 Review of National Programmes. Paris: OECD, 1984.

The overall report of the CRD assessment of 1983 reaffirms the budget constraints and their implications for energy RD&D activities. IEA expenditures declined by 6 percent in real terms. The total allocation amounted to U.S. $6.6 billion. To reduce dependence on foreign oil represents the most important energy policy objective of IEA Member Countries. The achievement of this objective differs between countries. Whatever the role of government, the focus is on industry with the task of commercializing new energy forms and technologies. Again, government involvement differs by country. Expenditures on conventional nuclear technology and government oil and gas technology development increased conservation technology; the share of IEA expenditures remained as is. The shares of coal, advanced nuclear, and renewable energies have decreased compared to 1982. Government expenditures on renewable energy technologies appear to be inversely related to the size of the economy. There is very limited information on energy RD&D programmes and budgets of private industry and this represents a serious constraint. Individual reports on twenty review countries are presented in the appendix.

149. Kendall, Jim. "The Bottom Line is Jobs - Labor and the Environmental Movement," Moving On, July - August, 1978, pp. 9-11; 21.

Organized labor has blessed the construction of nuclear power plants. The environmentalists fervently oppose it. The controversy centers around jobs. Local conferences have been organized between the two groups to discuss the matter. Corporate blackmail is practised to separate the two groups. The threat of job blackmail can be diffused by keeping the two groups informed of each others activities and programs. There are many common concerns between the two groups: health and safety of the workers, the survival of the cities and the corporate employers. The results of the conferences indicate a range from limited informal contacts to full-scale coalitions.

150. Koppel, Bruce and Schlegal, Charles. "Sociological Perspectives on Energy and Rural Development": A Review of Major Frameworks for Research on Developing Countries," Rural Sociology, Vol. 46, No. 2, 1981, pp. 203-219.

The contemporary energy situation raises new problems for rural development which require fresh thinking and perhaps some reorientation by sociologists. Five major frameworks for the sociological analysis of energy-rural development interactions in developing countries are critically evaluated. First, the socio-technical analysis is oriented to the decomposition of technological processes into basic tasks. Second, evolutionary perspectives identify systematic processes underlying the distribution of technologies and patterns of technology utilization across geographic, social and time considerations. Third, dependency focuses on the energy issue for the developing countries in the context of the international political economy. Fourth, the social impact analysis deals with performance indicators. Fifth, the ecological framework provides the energy accounting or the quantification of energy flows in all systems. The frameworks are evaluated in terms of their conceptualization of energy and its social significance, and the sociological variables emphasized. It is argued that energy reduction is a technological imperative with significant impact on the types of sociological analysis.

151. Lovejoy, Stephen B. "Energy Development and Employment Benefits: Who Gets the Jobs?" Thesis: Utah State University, 1980.

This study discusses the positive and negative effects associated with large-scale energy development projects when introduced in a rural region. It is argued that the rural residents may not receive the substantial direct employment benefits associated with such projects. It points out the negative effect of a rising crime rate, strains on the community services and facilities, environmental and social problems. The study evaluates the factors that affect the locals to obtain employment and to enhance their economic well-being. These cover the desire of the locals to seek the new positions, the number of local applicants, their socio-economic characteristics and occupational skills, and their actual hiring. The primary beneficiaries of a large-scale energy development will be the in-migrant construction workers and the citizens of the urban areas or the potential users of the energy generated by the project.

152. Marshall, Eileen and Robinson, Colin. The Economics of Energy Self-Sufficiency. British Institute's Joint Energy Policy Programme Energy Papers, No. 14. Brookfield, Vermont: Gower Publishing Company, 1984.

In this book the authors examine the influence which the desire for self-sufficiency has had on UK energy policy in the past and consider the feasibility of extending energy self-sufficiency as far ahead as 2020. Various policy approaches are described and, in the major part of the study, the authors examine in detail the perceived benefits which are explicit or implicit in the views of self-sufficiency advocates. They analyze whether energy supplies would be more secure, energy prices would be reduced, macroeconomic gains would appear and whether there might be advantages for distant generations. As well as evaluating potential benefits, the authors discuss the costs of prolonging self-sufficiency, such as the emergence of more monopolized and politicized energy market. (GWR)

153. Maxwell, Valerie. "Seabrook: A View From the Inside-Anti-Nuke Construction Worker Speaks out on Environment, Jobs, Unions," Seven Days, July 1978, pp. 23-24.

The article focuses on the Seabrook, New Hampshire protest over the construction of a nuclear power plant. The article is basically an interview with a construction worker at Seabrook. The Seabrook site would open up employment for workers from locals in New Hampshire, Maine, Rhode Island, and Massachusetts. The interviewed worker is fully aware of the nuclear controversy that nuclear energy is not the safest or cheapest type of energy. But, he has no choice with a family of 5 children. The unions continue to push nuclear plants for the sake of more jobs although the plants are dangerous. His opinion of union leaders is that they are distant and removed from the interests of the working people.

154. Mountain West Research, Inc. <u>Construction Worker Profile: Summary Report</u>. Billings, Montana: West Regional Commission, December 1975.

The report centers on the Rocky Mountain States which are the sites of major construction projects associated with the production of energy. This study evaluates the construction impacts on the area. It gathers information on construction projects and the work forces involved to document the sources of the resulting impacts and provide a comprehensive database. Three surveys were undertaken: 1) household (1400 households) 2) project (6000 workers) 3) community. A major impact is noted to a rise in the regional per capita income. The majority of the construction workers were similar in terms of socio-cultural background to the community residents. The workers were classified as local (39.9%) and non-local. About 46 percent of the non-local workers came from the same state. The effects of marital status, family size and presence/absence of family were examined. A demographic profile of the construction workers is presented in terms of age, education, income, labor force participation of spouses, and demand for housing. The effects of the construction projects on long-time residents is tackled by income, jobs and satisfaction with community services. The attitudes of long-term residents and newcomers were examined. Finally, the characteristics of the dependent population are studied.

155. Sachs, Ignacy. "Development Strategies with Moderate Energy Requirements: Problems and Approaches," <u>Cepal Review</u>, No. 12, April, 1981, pp. 103-109.

The paper outlines three dimensions of the energy crises. The first crisis discusses the limits to conventional energy resources (finiteness of planet). The implitation, here, is the survival of man depends on conservation and the development of renewable energy. The second crisis relates to the 'consumer society' as it evolved in the West and reached the third world countries (demonstration effect) resulting in the adoption of a very high capital intensive technology in the context of surplus labor and income inequality. The third dimension tackles the increase in the relative petroleum prices. The replacement process is viewed as costly because the new energy sources are considerably more expensive. Energy must be saved in all countries, including the major oil producers/exporters. It is important, therefore, to formulate development strategies with moderate energy resource requirements. Strategies to moderate demand include: elimination of waste,

improvement in the functioning of existing production and consumption systems, the restructuring of both systems, the exploration of
alternative means to meet the same social needs, and a change in
values or social demand.

Strategies regarding spatial organization and the readaptation of
transport systems are also considered.   To influence supply,
technological pluralism is offered to suit each region in terms of
economic and ecological effects. It is important to concentrate on
the relation between development and energy and to evaluate strategies in terms of their economic and ecological impacts.

156. Sansone, Paul. "Solar Utilization for Economic Development and
Employment in Low Income Communities (SUEDE)," Proceedings of Solar '79
Northwest, August 10-12, 1979 in Seattle, Washington.   Seattle,
Washington: U.S. Department of Energy, Bonneville Power Administration,
1979, pp. 106-109.

SUEDE was introduced to utilize low cost solar technology, to
assist the economic development of low income communities and to
encourage the disadvantaged individuals to participate.   The
duration of the project was three years. But, it was a short lived
solar program.   Serious institutional barriers obstructed its
proper implementation. Federal funding is not forthcoming with
funding delays. This was complicated by conflicting regulations,
and mid-stream changes in the CETA Title VI regulations. Federal
underfunding leads to intense competition that impedes low-cost
solar utilization. Implementation delays would result in high-tech
solutions. The recommended measures call for the confederation of
small organization and the adoption of a demonstration project.
The education of code enforcement officials in solar technologies
is a must. Once implemented, low cost solar applications are
positively supported by the public.

157. Susskind, Lawrence and O'Hare, Michael. Managing the Social and
Economic Impacts of Energy Development: Strategies for Facility Siting
and Compensating Impacted Communities and Individuals.   Cambridge,
Massachusetts: Massachusetts Institute of Technology, Laboratory of
Architecture and Planning, December 1977.

The study discusses the social and economic impacts of energy
development. The basic cause of energy boomtowns is energy development. The adverse effects include social disruption, public
service needs, shortage of private goods and services, inflation,
revenue shortfalls, and aesthetic deterioration.   Many of the
problems caused by energy development are aggravated by poor
facility siting decisions. Case studies of Wyoming, North Dakota,
Colorado and Texas provide insight at different approaches of
managing the social and economic adverse effects of energy development. It is important to estimate the social costs of energy
development and to compensate impacted individuals and communities.
Siting by auction is proposed i.e. and auction whereby local
governments compete for a proposed facility. It overcomes the
difficulties of figuring out the social costs associated with
energy development. The bidding process should be relegated to
local government, including the distribution of the compensation.

Residents and local officials can affect company decision—making by influencing its public image, shaping executives perceptions of the community by enacting regulations that speed or delay facility construction.

158. Vidyarthi, Varun. "Energy and the Poor in an Indian Village," World Development, Vol. 12, No. 8, 1984, pp. 821–836.

The study examines the energy problems of the rural poor associated with changes in the societal structure in a village in Northern India (Garhi). The fieldwork covered data collection (village census, agricultural survey, fuel survey, and discussion with villagers), as well as experimental introduction of alternatives (e.g. smokeless stoves and solar cookers). The paper provides a historical account of the villagers' fuel supplies in relation to the land tenure system and the corresponding social relations patterns. It examines the periods before and after "Zamindari", which reflects a proprietorship system of intermediaries between the state and the cultivators, and reviews the 1970 experience with the introduction of mechanization and land consolidation. Changes in the fuel consumption pattern of the poor tie with the changes in their economic opportunities and social relations. They relied on firewood at first as a cooking fuel. After the destruction of the forests by the Zamindars, the poor resorted to agricultural residues (cultivated land) and dung cakes (cattle). The advent of increasing mechanization and the reduced incidence of sharecropping or shift towards self—cultivation has led to significant changes in social relations in the extent of resource transactions between families of different classes. Contractual relationships replaced the patron—client relations. As a result, the landless and marginal landholders are turning to the use of harmful spring plants as cooking fuel. The future holds little promise for the poor in relation to energy supplies. The availability of fuels would be reduced substantially by the trend towards felling of orchards and shifts in cropping pattern. The alternatives (biogas, improved stoves, and tree plantation) are not forthcoming because of the poverty problem. Such investments were not perceived as worthwhile. Remedial energy action will not solve the problem unless tackled within a socioeconomic strategy to improve the well-being of the poor.

159. Von Lazar, Arpad and Magid, Bruce. "Energy Policy and Social Development: Notes on Trinidad-Tobago and Venezuela," Energy Policy, September 1975, pp. 201–210.

The article introduces the concept of energy havens to solve the problem of high wages alongside with unemployment in an open petroleum economy. The aim is to attract more labor—intensive industries than the petroleum sector. These are energy—intensive industries that use petroleum and natural gas as fuel or their derivatives as feedstock. They are, on average, 20–40 percent labor—intensive compared to the 0.7 percent labor-intensity of petroleum sector. The petrochemical industry is one industrial sector that would greatly benefit from an energy haven. Properly exploited, technology should provide expanded job opportunities to the benefit of lower income groups. The concept is applied to the cases of Trinidad-Tobago and Venezuela.

160. A Wall Street Journal News Roundup. "Soviet Disaster: Ukrainian Nuclear Fire Spreads Wide Tragedy With Radiation Cloud," The Wall Street Journal, Vol. CCVII, No. 84, April 30, 1986, pp. 1 and 24.

The nuclear accident in the Ukraine has damaged the nuclear power energy option. Loss of human life, injuries and serious environmental contamination resulted. All countries in the path of the released radiation have expressed great concern. The cause of the disaster was blamed on Russian design and management problems. The article compares the damaged reactor to the U.S. one, describes the operating reactors and those under construction around the world, and assesses the negative effects on the industry.

161. The World Bank. Renewable Energy Resources in the Developing Countries. Washington, D.C.: World Bank, January 1981.

The study examines the contributions that renewable resources can make to energy supplies in the developing countries. It discusses the role of the World Bank in renewable energy development in relation to the near future. The potential for the development of renewable energy is discussed in relation to the modern and traditional sectors wherein the latter, deforestation and soil erosion have contributed to desertification. Hence, the impact of renewable energy will be great for poor people. While many of these countries have favorable conditions to develop and use renewable energy, they still need to have our adequate data base to improve their technical talent, to formulate a deliverable system to reach a large number of users, and to provide an effective institutional arrangement for energy planning/implementation. The World Bank's role has been limited to lending for hydroelectric power and for fuelwood and forestry projects. For the next five years, the World Bank needs to concentrate on fuelwood and alcohol production projects. The Bank can also assist in terms of energy sector studies, institution building, research on appropriate technologies , and aid coordination. The study also surveys the renewable energy technologies that have the greatest potential to meet the energy needs of the developing nations. Three groups of technologies are examined: 1) for cooking in low-income households, 2) rural power technologies, 3) technologies for the modern sector.

162. Yanarella, Ernest J. and Yanarella, Anne-Marie (editors). "Energy Development in Kentucky: Its Impact Upon Community Life and Higher Education," Proceedings of a Symposium at the University of Kentucky March 28, 1979. Lexington, Kentucky: University of Kentucky, April, 1979.

This publication offers four presentations (plus a moderator) of a panel discussion on energy development in Kentucky and its impact on community life and higher education. The first presentation tackles the social, environmental and economic aspects of coal mining in Eastern Kentucky. The focus is on the new miner: the technologist. The second presentation recommends meeting the

social problems of the community by ascribing to the social responsibility doctrine for the corporations in this area to assist coal
mining and its workers. The third presentation reviews educational
programs offered to graduate trained personnel for coal mining.
The area needs more people to be involved in "make things happen"
in terms of better living conditions. The last presentation
emphasizes the bad living conditions in the area. Examples of
dreadful conditions of mountain roads, and flooding are given. The
lack of diversified economy is emphasized as well as certain
on-going practices are criticized (e.g. on-site construction
exemptions). The hope remains with the university to help.

5
Education, Training, and Manpower Development

---

163. Ackermann G.; Hampel R.; and Konschak, K. "Training of Industrial Engineers for Nuclear Power at the Training Reactor of the College of Advanced Technology Zittau." Paper presented at the International Atomic Energy Agency Symposium - Manpower Requirements and Development for Nuclear Programmes, Saclay, 2-6 April, 1979. Vienna: IAEA, 1980. IAEA-SM-238/7

> The light-water moderated 10 W training reactor of the College for Power Economy of the German Democratic Republic is presented. It serves for the training and continuation training of students and workers to be employed in nuclear power plant technology. Due to the one-year use of fresh fuel elements of a 10 MW research reactor and the selected design the reactor core great inherent nuclear safety and economy of operation are attained. Further characteristics of the training reactor are good accessibility of the interior of the core for in-core investigations, sufficient external experimental tunnels and a system of control, checking and protection which meets the requirements of the training programme. The technological and dosimetric equipment installed ensures not only reliable reactor operation but also extends experimental and training facilities as described in detail. In the final section the principles underlying the training programmes are explained by way of examples. The aim is for the training reactor to impart fundamental knowledge of processes in a nuclear power plant with a pressurized-water reactor. In cases where the behavior of a nuclear power plant cannot be sufficiently demonstrated by the training reactor, a reasonable supplementation of the training using especially developed simulation models and other experimental facilities has been conceived. (IAEA)

164. Ahmad, Yusuf J. Oil Revenues in the Gulf: A Preliminary Estimate of Absorptive Capacity. Paris: Organization for Economic Cooperation and Development, Development Centre, June 1974.

> The Gulf countries differ in relation to physical and human endowments, stages of development, monetary/financial structure and the overall approach to development. Such differences reflect on their degree of absorptive capacity and the associated problems. The countries could be broadly grouped into two. The first grouping

includes Iran, Iraq, Bahrain and Oman and shows little or no difficulty in finding outlets for their additional revenues. The second grouping covers Saudi Arabia, Kuwait, the United Arab Emirates and Qatar and depicts preoccupation with surplus income.

To enhance absorptive capacity requires massive investment in infrastructure and human resources development (education/training). There are basic limitations with such developments. As a result, productive investment has been concentrated in oil and oil-related industries. Viable projects in the area of water resources and agriculture (including food), aluminium, cement factories, electricity generation, and hotel construction represent viable investment targets. Telecommunications is also becoming an important investment field in the gulf.

165. Al-Abbas, Kasema A. and Moussa, H. M. "The Training and Development of the Workforce in the National Petroleum Industry," Oil and Development, Vol. 3, February 1978, pp. 18-34. (in Arabic)

The manpower development and training of the oil industry's work-force represent an important national issue for the oil-exporting countries. The study examines the characteristics of the workforce in companies in developing and training nationals. It discusses the experience of Iraq in that respect and the policies adopted by the foreign firms in the hiring of Iraqi workers in the petroleum industry. The manpower effects of nationalization and the shortage of skilled manpower to serve this industry are assessed. Finally, it relates the experience of Iraq National Oil Company in its efforts towards manpower development and training.

166. Alleyne, D.H.N. "The State Petroleum Enterprise and the Transfer of Technology." Paper presented at the United Nations Interregional Symposium on State Petroleum Enterprises in Developing Countries, Vienna, March 7-16, 1978, New York: Pergamon Press, 1980, pp. 109-122. ESA/NRET/AL. 11/13

This chapter discusses the issue of transfer of technology from the developed to the developing countries in the context of the petro-leum industry. There is an assymetric relationship or a typical developing country is totally technologically dependent which affects its economic development. For most developing countries, the technological process is one of acquiring a commercially feasible method, adapting it to their own environment, and applying scientific management. It is important for the developing world to be involved with the "rearrangement of prior knowledge" and to have persons "skilled in the prior art". The discussion focuses on the role of the state petroleum enterprises in the transfer of tech-nology. It is crucial for them to develop the right atmosphere and to train local personnel otherwise they will not be able to use the technology effectively and to achieve self-reliance. The United Nations can provide a list of firms owning/controlling various aspects of the petroleum technology. There is a need for an International Energy Institute. Only by training its personnel can these countries contribute to technological advances. It is essential, therefore , to create the institutions for the promotion of education and training in the natural sciences and in petroleum

technology.   There   is   room   for   cooperation   among   developing
countries in that respect.   The petroleum industry, if properly
developed, can be the basic point for the economy.

167. Arab   Labor   Organization.   Oil   and   Petrochemical   Labor   Office.
Labor and Planning in the Arab Petroleum Industries.   Baghdad, Iraq:
ALO, 1983. (in Arabic)

This article assesses the Arab countries in terms of their natural
and human resources.   In terms of natural resources, the Arab
countries are classified into three groups: 1) High or abundant
e.g., Saudi Arabia, 2) Medium e.g., Egypt, 3) Low or poor e.g.,
Syria.   The manpower situation of these countries is evaluated both
quantitatively and qualitatively.   The article surveys the population base of the Arab world, its labor supply potential and the
size of its workforce.   The educational attainment of the area
reflects 1) a high literacy rate estimated to be 65%, 2) low levels
of technical and vocational education.   In the light of this
presentation, the types of labor markets are examined in terms of
1) the informal sector, 2) the traditional sector, 3) the modern
sector.

With this background, the workforce characteristics of the petroleum industry are outlined first in general and then in reference
to the Arab countries.   It is reported that in the Arab oil
industry, the labor force suffers from low specialization, inadequate technical skills, and poor administrative talents.   Moreover,
manpower planning in that sector is very poorly handled as it is
only secondary to the financial strategy of any oil company.
Better utilization and reorganization are definitely highly needed.

168. Arab   Labor   Organization.   Oil   and   Petrochemical   Labor   Office.
Wages in the Oil and Chemical Sectors in the Context of Arab Laws.
Baghdad, Iraq: ALO, 1983. (in Arabic)

Wages in the oil and chemical sectors of the Arab World are
examined through a questionnaire prepared by the Labor Committee
for Oil and Chemicals. Wages are determined by individual or group
contracts.   The main objective is to point out the guarantees
specified in the laws to protect the workers of the industry.

169. Arora, S.C.; Bhutani, N.S.; and Raman, Rudha.   Manpower in the
Petroleum Sector.   Volume 1:   Refineries.   New Delhi, India: Institute
of Applied Manpower Research, 1977.

This report analyzes the employment pattern, education and
training, manpower policies and requirements for refineries in
India.   India has a refining capacity of 27.5 million tons per
annum with 10 refineries operating in different regions of the
country. The refining sector employed 18.76 percent in 1970, 19.84
percent in 1971 and 20.03 percent in 1972 of the total manpower
employed in the petroleum industry. The idea is to develop guidelines and prepare a set of manning matrices to be used for forecasting manpower training and development requirements of manpower
to meet the primary needs of the sector. Long-term forecasting is
essential to take into account replacement, expansion and turnover

needs. It was found out that there was a high degree of imbalance of technically qualified persons. The manpower policies (salaries, incentives, recruitment, promotion working hours) were not uniform. The training facilities need to be geared to meet the new demands arising out of reorienting work organization practices by implementing the multi-craft concept. It is suggested that a cadre of polycraft technicians on maintenance be developed by all refineries. A comprehensive information system to be used at different management levels for evaluating the effectiveness of maintenance basis has been neglected and needs to be developed.

170. Asian Development Bank. Asian Energy Problems. New York: Preager Publishers, 1982.

The Asian Development Bank (ADB) has been conscious of the changing world energy situation since 1973 and its implications for all aspects of economic and social development of its Developing Member Countries (DMCs). As a result, the Regional Energy Survey (RES) was designed to study the energy situation in greater depth in order to set priorities regarding future, energy-related assistance to the DMCs. This report analyzes the energy situation for the DMCs excluding India. The report examines the past demand and supply of energy trends up to 1978 and discusses policy issues of energy pricing, conservation and interfuel substitution. Special consideration was given to the rural energy supplies and perspective energy demand projections were made on a country by country basis and by energy source up to the year 1990. Potential indigenous supply sources as well as energy imports were projected for the same period. On the basis of these estimates, energy-related investments and the foreign exchange needs for energy imports are projected. A major constraint with respect to achieving self-reliance is the lack of appropriately trained manpower in the DMCs. To aim at increasing self-reliance requires the necessary human resources to design and execute appropriate energy policies and programs. Self-reliance in software capability would call for large increases in the manpower requirements with appropriate skills to manage the construction and production of the energy industry as well as the manpower to evaluate the energy situation and design optimal sector strategies. Few DMCs have assessed the manpower needs for energy development. It is important to undertake a continuous effort towards appropriate training by organized interaction of the energy planners of the various DMCs.

171. Badre, Albert Y. and Siksek, Simon G. Manpower and Oil in Arab Countries. Lebanon, Beirut: Economic Research Institute, American University of Beirut, 1959.

Manpower problems arising from the entry of the oil industry into the Arab World have been the central object of investigation of this study. Three main sources are identified 1) The nature of the oil industry, 2) the lifestyle transition from an agricultural-pastoral society to an industrial one, and 3) the dynamic evolution of the Arab Society driven by native and foreign socio-political forces. The countries under review are Iraq, Kuwait, Saudi Arabia and Syria. Four issues are specifically addressed. First, the building of an effective labor force is discussed in terms of recruitment and training. Three factors influence the recruitment policies of the oil companies operating in these Arab countries: 1) terms of concession agreements, 2) laws and regulations in Arab countries, 3) characteristics of labor markets. Training is vital not only as a means of increasing the productive capacity of local workers but also as a source of accumulation of strategic human resources that are so critical to the future development of these countries. The general conditions of employment are presented in terms of labor force classification, wages, hours of work, benefit plans.

Second, the development of managerial resources emphasises the key role of the foreign manager in the various programs instituted by the oil companies towards this goal. The burden of training and preparing nationals for responsible positions falls on him. Third, the handling of labor management relations pertains to the responses which labor makes to the challenge of industrial life and to the handling of these responses by management and other institutions. Turnover and absenteeism has been remarkably low compared to other industries and regions. Fourth, the effects of the interaction between the industry and its environment upon the development of manpower resources. The oil industry is alien to society. There have been attempts at a policy of integration. Oil companies are required by government to look to government local offices as agencies representing workers. The government attempts to contain and control labor protest in oil companies by approving laws and practices designed to help for greater labor satisfaction and higher standards of living. There is pressure now to publicize the resolutions by regional/international agencies.

172. Barker, Helen. Investigation of Labor, Manpower, and Training Requirements for Selected Solar Applications - Technical Progress Report. Golden, Colorado: SERI, January 1978.

This study reviews the programs addressing labor, manpower, and training requirements of selected solar energy technologies, identifies the barriers in these programs and recommends a research program for selected solar energy technologies. The potential of solar energy is still untapped. The commercialization potential for the use of solar energy in space heating, combined heating and cooling of buildings and hot water heating seems relatively high and would have significant contributions in the next decade or so. Their manufacturing is well developed, but their distribution, installation and services still drag. This may be due to the lack of trained personnel for the diffusion of the technology. Other solar technologies (e.g. wind energy, photovoltaic, and biomass energy conversion systems) are still at the development level and the corresponding manpower requirements focus on engineering and scientific areas. The study outlines the methodology or list of tasks that need to be undertaken in order to improve information on labor, manpower and training issues. For example, definition of universe of organizations, employment data by occupation and skill levels, demand for technicians, creation of appropriate occupational titles, labor intensiveness of different systems, development of training curricula, geographical dispersion of technical labor force and labor organization.

173. Becker, David L. "The Future-Career Opportunities for Engineering Graduates in the Power Industry." Paper presented at the 1981 ASEE Annual Conference-Education and Industry: A Joint Endeavor. Washington, D.C.: The American Society for Engineering Education, 1981, Vol. 3, pp. 969-973.

Power (energy) engineer will be in high demand in the 1980's. The paper presents the factual reasons behind the need for power engineers by industry. It is recommended to change the terminology from power to Energy engineer. There is a significant projected increase in the price of barrel oil through year 2000. The increase in the costs of energy lead to a higher demand for power engineers. It is also associated with the retirement of a large number of engineers hired during the 1945-50 period. If supply will not respond, industry will be forced to hire from other engineering disciplines. Enrollment in electrical/engineering is projected to increase until 1985 and to decline after that. A 12.5 percent increase in graduates was experienced between 1979 and 1980. Yet, industry's needs were up 29 percent for that same year. Students have been discouraged from majoring in that area in favor of electronics, digital computers, and microwave. The enrollment of foreign students who typically return home have denied admission to qualified U.S. students. The demand of industry should be on the rise. The implementation of nuclear programs would call for 46,000 new engineers by year 2000. The synfuel production target of 1990 would require an additional 25,000 engineers. The Mx missile program would also create a large need for engineers. In addition, emerging areas (cogeneration, coal gasification, transmission, biomass, load management, geothermal, solar and wind, distribution, and hydro-generation) would require more power engineers. The field of power engineering is alive and has great future prospects. It is important, therefore, to 1) develop a solid curriculum, 2) integrate the efforts of academia and industry, 3) provide financial support and supportive services, 4) use industry staff in the classroom, 5) develop a continuing education program for the working engineers.

174. Blair, L. M. and Doggette, J. "Education, Training and Work Experience Among Nuclear Power Plant Workers." Paper presented at the International Atomic Energy Agency Symposium - Manpower Requirements and Development for Nuclear Programmes, Salary, 2-6 April, 1979. Vienna: IAEA, 1980. IAEA-SM-238/22

The paper uses a unique data set to examine the prior work experience, training and education of skilled and technical workers in United States nuclear power plants. The data were collected in the latter half of 1977 by the International Brotherhood of Electrical Workers (IBEW) in a survey of union locals in nuclear power plants. The survey results provided substantial evidence that workers in United States nuclear power plants have a relatively high level of education, training, and skill development. Analysis of average education by age did not reveal any significant differences in years of schooling between younger and older workers. Very high rates of participation in formal training programme was held on-site at the power plant and was provided by utility personnel. The majority of workers reported previous work experience related to nuclear power plant activities. Almost one-third of the workers had been directly involved in nuclear energy in a previous job, the majority of these through the United States Navy nuclear programme. However, the newer plants are hiring relatively fewer persons with previous nuclear experience. (IAEA)

175. Burns, Barbara; Mason, Bert; and Armington, Keith. The Role of Education and Training Programs in the Commercialization and Diffusion of Solar Energy Technologies. Golden, Colorado: Solar Energy Research Institute, January 1979. SERI/RR-53-128

An important part of analyzing employment and labor force requirements in the solar energy field is determining the availability of trained and experienced workers and of programs to provide additional training. This paper provides a base for the analysis of these labor force supply questions by identifying the importance of education and training in the commercialization and diffusion of solar technologies, discussing issues for planning and analysis of solar education and training efforts, and illustrating the range of programs and courses presently available. The paper reviews four general perspectives on the diffusion of a new technology such as solar energy systems, with special attention to the education and training issues. Planning and analysis issues discussed included: whether there is a need for more education and training programs, and of what kinds; the possible roles of the federal and state governments; the tradeoffs between expanding the capabilities of persons already within the HVAC field or training unemployed and underemployed persons as solar workers; and the allocation of effort between training workers and training trainers. Examples of programs and courses are given for the four categories identified: general education, professional solar energy education and training, technician training, and solar industries infrastructure training. The general conclusion is that a large number and variety of education and training programs and courses are presently offered, but that little or no evaluation of individual programs or the overall effort has yet been done.

176. Cakici, M. H. "The Turkish Nuclear Power Project – Manpower Development and Personnel Planning for Operation and Maintenance." Paper presented at the International Atomic Energy Agency Symposium – Manpower Requirements and Development for Nuclear Programmes, Saclay, 2-6 April, 1979. Vienna: IAEA, 1980. IAEA-SM-238/16

This paper presents the Turkish Electricity Authority's current policy and approach to manpower development for its nuclear power project, particularly as regards the project team and operation group. The existing staff consists of 40 technical employees in the project team and a proposed organization chart illustrates that about 110 technical staff are needed for operation and maintenance of the power plant. The strategy to meet the necessary and urgent manpower requirements and the availability of training facilities are discussed. The paper evaluates training possibilities both in Turkey and abroad and, in addition, gives a provisional training schedule for the operation and maintenance group. (IAEA)

177. Collier, Hugh. <u>Developing Electric Power - Thirty Years of World</u> <u>Bank Experience</u>. Washington, D.C.: The International Bank for Reconstruction and Development. The World Bank, 1984.

> The objective of the book is a review of the lending policies of the World Bank for electric power development and assessment of the results. At first, a general description of the Bank's activities and choice of projects for lending is given. Then, the financial policies are examined in terms of power tariffs, utility rates and economic efficiency. Cases of countries with financial diffi- culties are discussed (India, Mexico, Indonesia, Turkey, Argentina, and Uruguay). Issues of investment planning and project implemen- tation, as well as the involvement of the bank with projects for rural electrification are examined. The starting point of all appraisals for power projects is an estimate of future demand. The execution of projects is assessed in terms of costs and timing. Of special significance is the institutional development analysis in the power industry. The bank has encouraged and assisted in the establishment of autonomous power agencies. It is maintained that the agency should have competent management with a high degree of continuity. At the same time, the agency should have the authority to set wages and salaries to attract and retain staff. The short- age of skilled and experienced personnel is more pronounced in low-income countries. There are opportunities for the bank to assist with training problems. The bank has a definite interest in the consultants and contractors employed on projects it finances. Their choice should be acceptable to the bank. In the eighties, the extent to which the bank will be able to continue or expand its operations remains to be seen. But, there is a definite need for the Bank's financial and nonmonetary contributions. Country summaries (Pakistan, Singapore, Taiwan, Ghana, Kenya, Nigeria, Egypt, Iran, Tunisia, Bolivia, Ecuador and Peru) are presented in the Appendix.

178. Combe, J. "Organization de la Formation et Methodes Pedagogues a Electricite de France." Paper presented at the <u>International Atomic</u> <u>Energy Agency Symposium - Manpower Requirements and Development for</u> <u>Nuclear Programmes</u>, Saclay, 2-6 April, 1979. Vienna: IAEA, 1980. IAEA-SM-238/38 (in French)

> The training of staff for the equipping, operating and servicing of EDF nuclear facilities was organized at a time when the undertaking had already developed its general training schemes and teaching methods. A brief account of these schemes and methods is given in the paper. Staff training at EDF was clearly devised with implicit regard for the educational and technological features of French society. This fact should not be forgotten when seeking to compare what is described here with developments abroad. The organization of training is not just knowledge, and this calls for a combination of teaching and practical experience. Training programmes are drawn up taking into account the professional experience acquired in a particular trade, and training activities are, as far as possible, divorced from selection and examination procedures. The large number of workers needing to be trained in the nuclear field has led to standardization of training programmes. Teaching methods tend to be based on a combination of theoretical instruc-

tion and practical experience. Training thus involves the use of active or semi-active methods designed to promote familiarization with methods of working as well as the attainment of knowledge and ability. For these reasons, conditions of training as close as possible to actual work situations are created in the training centers, where great emphasis is placed on simulation techniques. (IAEA)

179. Densmore, Raymond E. The Coal Miner of Appalachia. Parsons, West Virginia: McClain Printing Company, 1977.

This short exposition is a first-hand account about mining in the bituminous coal beds of western Maryland, southwestern Pennsylvania and Northern West Virginia. The author (an old miner) gives a detailed picture of the working conditions in the mines from 1914 to 1974. The story describes the changes in hiring practices, safety measures and training procedures used during these times.

180. DeVuono, Anthony C.; Don W.; and Hajek, Brian J. "University Programs for Improving the Technical Capability of Nuclear Power Plant Operations Personnel." Paper presented at the 1981 ASEE Annual Conference-Education and Industry: A Joint Endeavor. Washington, D.C.: The American Society for Engineering Education, 1981, Vol. 3, pp. 1058-1063.

The paper recommends that nuclear power plant personnel be required to complete specific university courses to enhance their technical capabilities for plant site performance. It, specifically, addresses four issues. First, the educational program should satisfy the needs of the participants, and of the utility as well as meet the regulatory requirements of the Nuclear Regulatory Commission on site course offerings are recommended. Second, there should not be any trade-off between the program and on-the-job performance. Also education requirements should not obstruct occupational mobility and place secondary emphasis on plant specific training and in-plant experience. A Bachelor of Science degree in Engineering is preferred to the Bachelor of Engineering Technology. The educational program for plant personnel must be flexible. At the same time, close interaction with university faculty would prove beneficial. Third, a detailed outline of the major educational program elements is presented covering english and communications, engineering technical courses, basic education requirement courses, and full electives. The engineering technical courses are discussed in relation to the senior reactor operator and the shift technical advisor. The fourth issue deals with how to alleviate the constraints (costs and approval) of implement-ation. Basic courses in mathematics, physics, engineering, and chemistry should be taught by faculty from junior colleges or technical schools nearby plant. The advanced engineering courses would be taught by faculty from a university offering a B.S. degree in Engineering. Quality assurance and geographic coverage are important consideration for the Board of Regents in relation to off-campus instruction. Finally, the paper proposes a program of reciprocal transfer of credit between a two-year and a four-year institution. The Associate of Arts Degree could serve as a pre-engineering component to a B.S. M.E. Degree. Such education programs are expected to significantly improve the capabilities and opportunities of Nuclear Power Plant Operations Personnel.

181. Doggette, John R. Energy-Related Technology Programs in Community and Junior Colleges: An Analysis of Existing and Planned Programs. Oak Ridge, Tennessee: Oak Ridge Associated Universities, July 1976.

The study surveys 1152 institutions (junior, community, and technical, colleges) during the period October 1975 to January 1976 to determine the number of existing and planned energy-related occupational technology programs, to estimate the degree and type of cooperation between the colleges and energy industries and to quantify the degree of interest in the attendance of a working conference, to assess occupational needs in energy as well as initiate the planning of needed programs. The research design and methodology is outlined. The results indicate a total of 76 existing energy programs and 158 new planned ones. Public colleges are much more involved than private colleges in energy related technology programs covering petroleum (oil and gas), coal-mining, nuclear energy, solar energy, laser-optics, geothermal energy, and energy conservation. The responding colleges maintained that energy-related occupational needs will reflect the nation's response to energy demands. At present, at the macro level, a very small percentage of workers are employed or trained in energy-extraction or energy-production industries. It is important for them to be aware of the energy needs in their geographical regions.

182. Duiker, Peter. "Manpower Analysis for the Energy Sector, Some Macro Issues for Discussion." Paper presented at Expert Group Meeting on Assessment of Manpower and Training Needs for the Energy Sector, Bangkok, Thailand, 8-10 December 1982. Geneva, Switzerland: ILO, November 1982. ESCAP/UNDP/ILO/UNESCO

The analysis of the human resource factor in the energy sector has been scanty. The present discussion paper summarizes the main issues in manpower analysis, in particular as it applies to planning for energy development programmes as well as to the implementation and the monitoring of human resources aspects for sectoral investment actions. In addition, proposals are made for a work programme for energy manpower analysis for those countries interested in implementing effective energy action plans. Three main approaches to manpower analysis are reviewed and evaluated: the manpower requirements, the cost-benefit, and labor market information approach. The characteristics of the energy sector relevant to manpower assessments are discussed. The massive investments, the drive to improve productivity, the diversified nature and low level of sectoral integration represent some of the general traits of the energy sector which dictate the type of manpower analysis to be effectively applied. Finally, it is argued that manpower analysis should not be carried out in isolation from the overall social aspects of alternative energy development strategies. At the same time, social progress will be influenced by the energy policy adopted. The ILO has important contributions to make to human resources implications of alternative energy options. Three areas are specified: methodology of energy assessments, development of an energy manpower data base and participation in energy sector surveys.

183. Duiker, Peter. <u>Manpower Implications of Accelerated Energy Resource Development in Developing Countries.</u> Geneva, Switzerland: International Labour Office, September 1983.

This paper examines the manpower implications of accelerated energy resource development in developing countries. Three major aspects are discussed: 1) the manpower constraints in the energy development process, 2) the actions necessary to attract and retain qualified manpower, and 3) the priorities for energy manpower policy in developing countries. The conclusions emerging from this study provides more realistic expectations of the contribution of manpower planning to sectoral development. This paper suggests that experience appears to justify manpower analysis and monitoring for energy sub-sectors. However, this must be concluded with an overall program for the entire energy sector in order to be effective. If energy manpower analysis becomes part of a systematic approach, it can aid in the minimization of bottlenecks in resource development. A prevalent constraint found is the lack of adequate data.

184. Duncan, Shelby and Mahoney, James. <u>Energy-Related Activities in Community, Junior and Technical Colleges: A Directory.</u> Washington, D.C.: American Association of Community and Junior Colleges Energy Communications Center, May 1981.

The involvement of two-year colleges in energy programming has been significant over the last few years. About 1,425 programs are offered at present. About 67 percent of the two-year colleges in the United States offer energy instruction or implement some kind of energy conservation policies. There is clear indication that energy education programs would expand even more in the future. This would occur in the less-than-degree/certificate programs. The concentration interim of energy areas would be in nuclear, coal, conservation petroleum, and environmental. This publication represents a comprehensive resource text. It lists college, program focus, activity breakdown, contact information/person and references, if any.

185. Eckman, Tom. "Seattle/OIC's Solar Training and Curriculum Development Program," <u>Proceedings of Solar '79 Northwest, August 10-12, 1979, Seattle, Washington.</u> Seattle, Washington: U.S. Department of Energy, Bonneville Power Administration, 1979, pp. 317-319.

Seattle Opportunities Industrialization Center (Seattle/OIC) is a community based, non-profit vocational training and job placement organization. Its primary purpose is to counsel, train and place economically disadvantaged individuals into entry-level occupations. Present curriculum offerings include carpentry, plumbing and pipefitting, electrical maintenance and eight other areas.

Since the Spring of 1978, Seattle/OIC has been engaged in two research and curriculum development projects related to decentralization renewable energy technologies. The purpose of these projects has been to 1) assess the employment potential resulting from the deployment of solar energy systems in Washington State and

2) to develop an appropriate vocational curriculum to use in training individuals to fill those solar related jobs. A survey of the existing solar industry in Washington State and a formal labor market analysis for the Seattle/King County area were prepared. These studies revealed that there is sufficient demand for solar systems to warrant the mounting of vocational training programs provided that: 1) the programs augment training in the existing building trades, 2) concentrate on energy conservation, domestic hot water systems, passive space heating technologies, and
3) do not attempt to train highly specialized "solar technicians." Moreover, the expanded use of solar technologies could increase the demand for craft workers in the Seattle/King County area by as much as one-third by 1986. (BPA)

186. Egnor, Terry L. and Armstrong, Richard. "Solar Greenhouse Construction: A Model for Energy Education," Proceedings of Solar '79 Northwest, August 10-12, 1979 in Seattle, Washington. Seattle, Washington: U.S. Department of Energy, Bonneville Power Administration, 1979, pp. 313-316.

Educational programs could increase the students' awareness of energy/environment issues. This paper reflects the experience with a pilot program for active involvement with energy problems by the Bush School Environmental Research and Learning Center (ERLC). Solar greenhouses were constructed for the fourth grade classroom containing an active/passive solar heating system calculated to provide 75 percent of the heat. The school dependence on fuel oil declined. The project represents a typical example of energy conservation at work and the use of renewable energy. The project serves as a model (showcase prototype) for the community.

187. El Watari, Abdel Aziz. "The Labor Force Needs of the OAPEC Member Countries," OAPEC Bulletin, October 1978, pp. 22-29. (in Arabic)

The total number of workers in the oil sector of the OAPEC member countries is estimated to be 200,000 and represents only 1% of their aggregate workforce. A preliminary study undertaken by the organization revealed the need to train a minimum of 100,000 individuals for the oil sector. The significance of this pool is particularly felt for those states that mostly rely on foreign labor. Three levels of skills are indicated: 1) high skills or university graduates, 2) technical and supervising skills or high school graduates, and 3) skilled workers with intermediate education. Two important findings need special emphasis. The first relates to the underutilization of capacity at some training centers in certain countries that could be used by other member countries. The second stresses the lack of a standard training programme for the development of training instructors and personnel.

188. Ericson, Katherine. The Solar Jobs Book. Andover, Massachusetts: Brickhouse Publishing Company, 1980.

The solar industry and the number of people working in it is growing rapidly in response to three significant trends: 1) use of government incentives, 2) increases in the costs of fossil fuels,

and 3) decreases in the costs of solar energy systems. It is clear
that the development of energy conservation measures and solar
technologies will create jobs. After discussing the new breed of
workers in solar energy and the solar jobs in traditional settings
like private corporations, trades, government, public schools, and
colleges, the book offers a directory of resources for information,
jobs and education in solar energy. Eleven listings are given that
represent key directories in the field. This is followed by a
listing of the professional trade, and other non-profit organizations that provide useful sources of general information about
solar activity in different geographic localities.

189. Garey, R. B.; Bell, Sharon E.; and Lee, Howard. Supplemental
Tables: Doctoral Scientists and Engineers Working in Energy-Related
Activities, 1979. Washington, D.C.: U.S. Department of Energy, June
1982. ORAU-200 (NTIS)

   This volume of tables is a supplement to Doctoral Scientists and
   Engineers Working in Energy-Related Activities, 1979. The tables
   provide information on the number of energy-related doctoral
   scientists and engineers in 1979. The data consist of:
   1. The degree and employment fields of PhDs working in
       energy-related activities
   2. Type of employer, energy source, and work activity
   3. Trends in U.S. government funding of energy-related PhDs
   4. Degree, employment fields and geographical distribution of
       1977-78 PhD graduates.

190. Harman, Henry V. "Creative Grantsmanship for Municipal Energy
Conservation," in Gregory A. Danake and George K. Lagassa (editors).
Energy Policy and Public Administration. Lexington, Massachusetts: D.C.
Heath and Company, 1980, pp. 97-105.

   This writing shows how municipalities can use creative grantsmanship to defray some of the costs of energy conservation. Examples
   are given of municipal projects which have combined these grants
   with federal funding for community and human resource development.
   An example of this concept combines employment programs with energy
   conservation. This program, called the "Solar Utilization/Economic
   Development and Employment Program" (SUEDE), provides training and
   employment for low-income individuals while demonstrating the
   feasibility of solar water heating systems. Successfully funded
   SUEDE projects have been implemented throughout the United States.
   The author points out that these types of programs should be
   considered as vehicles in applying human energy to solve our total
   energy problems.

191. Holloway, F.A.L. " A View of the Effect of Oil Industry Divestiture
on Science and Technology," in David J. Teece (editor). R & D in
Energy. Stanford, California: Institute for Energy Studies, August
1977. pp. 213-229.

   The study tackles the effects of divestiture on the scientific and
   technological activities of a typical petroleum corporation such as
   Exxon. Divestiture (both vertical and horizontal) was contemplated
   in two proposed legislations: Petroleum Industry Competition Act

(1976) and Interfuel Competition Act (1975). The first would require reorganization so that exploration and production, transportation, and refining and marketing operations would be separately owned and managed. The second would exclude oil companies from participating in the development of non-oil energy sources.

The technology development and innovation system of an integrated company such as Exxon is highly competitive. To break it down into smaller units would result in reduced domestic energy development that would push up oil prices and hurt the public. Its manpower structure includes 12,000 technical employees (scientists, engineers and technicians). About 5,000 are working in research (19) and engineering (5) centers. The rest are with the operating divisions and affiliates. There are more than 800 individuals holding doctoral degrees. Such a human resource base may not have the same career options or competitive choices if the government should take over a significantly greater role in what has been privately financed R & D to meet civilian needs in the energy field. Moreover, government funded R & D has not been successful in developing processes, products or systems to satisfy the market needs of the general public. It has a good record only where the government is the customer.

192. International Atomic Energy Agency. Manpower Development for Nuclear Power: A Guidebook. Technical Reports Series No. 200. Vienna: International Atomic Energy Agency, September 1980.

This guidebook provides policy-makers and managers of nuclear power programmes with information and guidance on the role, requirements, planning and implementation of manpower development programmes. This publication is suitable to any economic setting and is of great relevance to the developing countries of the world where manpower represents a critical constraint. The outline followed is divided into three parts: 1) manpower requirements, 2) national participation and manpower development, and 3) manpower development for a nuclear power programme. It also offers a bibliography on the subject matter. The first topic offers detailed information on the activities and tasks (pre-project and project implementation) to be performed, the number of persons needed and their qualifications. In the second part, the guidebook discusses the purpose, scope, benefits, limitations and policies, of national participation. The experiences of seven member states are given. The manpower development programme elements are tackled in terms of the assessment of national education requirements and their potential, the national training resources and foreign options, as well as the programme scheduling and implementation procedures. It is emphasized that efforts are needed to ensure the retention of trained manpower and the provision of good working conditions.

193. International Atomic Energy Agency. Manpower Requirements and Development for Nuclear Power Programmes. Proceedings of An International Symposium Held by the International Atomic Energy Agency at Saclay, 2-6 April 1979. Vienna: International Atomic Energy Agency, 1980.

A collection of papers is presented in the proceedings of the International Symposium on Manpower Requirements and Development

for Nuclear Power Programmes held by the International Atomic
Energy Agency (IAEA).   After discussing the general aspects of
manpower requirements, the national experiences and manpower
development programmes are reviewed.   International assistance in
training is also tackled.   A total of 38 papers covering 14
countries are presented.   It is clear that the supply of qualified
manpower is a prerequisite to successful implementation.   Installed
nuclear capacity is expected to increase by one-third.   That
translates itself into the need for more than 100,000 persons to
receive specialized training.   Foreign assistance may be needed to
fill in for the lack of domestic training opportunities.

194. International Labour Organization.   Manpower Assessment and
Planning Projects in the Arab Region: Current Issues and Perspectives.
Geneva, Switzerland: International Labour Organization, 1979.

This is a review of the manpower assessment and planning projects
undertaken by the ILO in Arab countries since the early sixties.
It critically analyzes the performance of these projects in
relation to their stated objectives and contribution to human
resource development.   A major weakness found was the lack of
reference to labour markets.   In response to this weakness an
analysis of the current main characteristics of the Arab labour
markets is provided.   This evaluation divides the Arab region into
two distinct states: capital-rich (the oil exporters) and capital-
poor.   The review of the capital-rich states shows that these
countries experience a qualitative and quantitative dependence on
migrant labour.   The implications and effects of these migrant
workers on the labour market is described.   Finally, the study
provides a regional manpower planning programme which suggests the
capital-rich states can prevent manpower bottlenecks, institute an
effective immigration policy, educate and motivate the national
workplace and encourage participation of women in the workplace.

195. Kanter, M.S.   "Training of Nuclear Power Professionals in
International Courses."   Paper presented at the International Atomic
Energy Agency Symposium - Manpower Requirements and Development for
Nuclear Programmes, Saclay, 2-6 April, 1979.   Vienna: IAEA, 1980.
IAEA-SM-238/20

Argonne National Laboratory has presented nine international
courses in the IAEA Nuclear Power Training Programme.   Five have
been overview courses fifteen weeks in length and four have been
specialized courses ranging from five to nine weeks.   A total of
286 participants from 38 countries have been trained in these
courses.   The Argonne courses comprise approximately 40 percent of
the Agency's programme, which is also carried out in France, Spain,
and the Federal Republic of Germany.   The two types of overview
courses, one covering the planning phase of a project and the other
the construction and operation phase, surveyed all aspects of
nuclear power programmes - economic, managerial, regulatory, and
technical.   Experience has shown that the majority of the participants in those courses had concentrated interest in specialized
areas.   Specialized courses have now been offered on five specific
subjects.   Based on past course evaluations by our staff, 37
percent of those trained were judged capable of making significant

contribution to their country's nuclear programme; 44 percent were judged potentially capable of such contributions; 17 percent were capable of only limited contribution; and 2 percent were inappropriately selected. We have found a vast variation in the way participating countries select applicants for the course. Participation in international training has been very useful because of the exposure to working experts and because of the interaction between participants from the different developing countries. It is clear that such courses of moderate length sometimes attract senior management personnel, but in general can best be directed to responsible staff at middle management levels. More junior staff would be more effectively trained at the national level. Preliminary results of a Center survey of those participants who were trained two years ago have confirmed these conclusions. (IAEA)

196. Little, Joanne R. and Shirley, Duveen, L. Nuclear Engineering Enrollments and Degrees, 1981. Washington, D.C: U.S. Department of Energy, May 1982. ORAU--199, DE82 014883 (NTIS)

This report presents data on the number of students enrolled and the degrees awarded in academic year 1980-81 from 73 U.S. institutions offering degree programs in nuclear engineering or nuclear options within other engineering fields. Presented here are historical data for the last decade, which provide information such as trends by degree level, foreign national student participation, female and minority student participation, and placement of graduates. Also included is a listing of the universities by type of program and number of students. (ORAU)

197. Mahmoud, Fahmi. "Foundation and Development of Petroleum Cadres," Petroleum, Vol. 16, No.5, 1979, pp. 53-55. (in Arabic)

This short article tackles the development of the workforce in the oil industry of Egypt. It offers both short range and long range plans. It proposes an individual short-term approach for managerial posts. For long-term planning, it distinguishes between a) general training covering the middle level skills, b) specific training covering the university graduates and c) training positions with limited contract and in accordance with a set programme.

198. Mautner - Markhof, F. "Manpower Development for Nuclear Power." Paper presented at the International Atomic Energy Agency Symposium - Manpower Requirements and Development for Nuclear Programmes, Saclay, 2-6 April, 1979. Vienna: IAEA, 1980. IAEA-SM-238/25

The necessity and importance of manpower development for nuclear power programmes is becoming increasingly recognized by both the developing and developed Member States of the Agency. It is generally agreed that there is a very widespread and large underestimation of the need and numbers of highly qualified manpower required to ensure the safety and reliability of nuclear power, and of the economic and social consequences of the lack of such manpower. There is a fundamental need for and responsibility of a developing country to provide, at the outset of a nuclear power project, the national organization and resources for planning and implementing a manpower development programme. The basic considerations which go into manpower planning and implementation are discussed, in particular the factors influencing a manpower development programme and the need for a core of indigenous qualified manpower from the beginning of planning a nuclear power project, even if it is a turn-key project. Indigenous manpower that has both the technical expertise and extensive knowledge of local conditions is best equipped to adapt successfully imported nuclear power technology to the needs of a developing country, thus providing increased self-sufficiency as well as safe and reliable nuclear power. Also discussed are: the general nature of the interface between manpower development and national participation; education and on-the-job training; manpower requirements for a nuclear power project; and manpower for a nuclear regulatory body. IAEA activities in manpower development which are discussed include: the IAEA Guidebook on Manpower Development for Nuclear Power; the IAEA Programme of Training Courses in Nuclear Power; on-the-job training; and the IAEA Fellowship Programme. (IAEA)

199. Mikalonis, Saulius. "Solar Training," _Sun Times_, May/June, 1983, pp. 6-7.

The solar heating industry offers an alternative to the unemployed from the auto and steel industries. Sales of solar collectors increased significantly between 1975-1981. Solar water heaters were installed in many more buildings. The solar construction provides four times as many jobs as an equal investment in electric and gas utilities. The growth potential and labor-intensiveness is great. The National Association of Home Builders (NAHB) in conjunction with Job Corps offers a solar training program. Ninety-seven persons graduated from the solar installation program in its first two years and has 120 enrollees at present. Employers who hire trainees receive a 50 percent federal tax credit on $600 wages paid during the first year of employment and 25 percent credit in the second year. A 90 percent placement rate is maintained. The curriculum includes hands-on training in addition to classroom instruction. Federal support for Job Corps is needed and is worth it for a promising new industry.

200. Moore, Allen B. Energy Problems Provide Job Opportunities. Washington, D.C.: U.S. Department of Health Education and Welfare, Bureau of Occupational and Adult Education, July 1, 1977. ED142794 (ERIC)

This report focuses on the linkage between vocational education and energy. The occupations related to the development of alternative energy sources are identified as well as its implications for vocational education. The potential areas of employment are grouped under a) home and industry, b) transportation, and c) policy decision-making. The first area appears to show the highest potential for training and employment opportunities. It is believed that conservation practices can lead to expanding occupational opportunities. Service areas of home economics, agriculture, business, and office occupations would receive the most attention for conservation efforts. Vocational education help is unlimited. A list of conservation activities is outlined by service area.

201. Mostafa, Mohamed K. "Coordination Efforts Towards the Development of Needed Manpower for the Construction, Operation and Maintenance of the Arab Petrochemical Industry," Arab Industrial Development, No. 26, April 1976, pp. 65-72. (in Arabic)

> This paper discusses the labor problems in the Arab petrochemical industry. It examines the importance of labor relative to the other factors of production in the context of the industry. Labor is considered a scarce resource in the Arab labor market. The paper compares the characteristics of the workforce relative to other traditional industries. It also tackles the issue of developing the needed manpower structure including the formation of local supervisors to deal with the foreign companies that handle the construction task. Finally, the paper emphasizes the need for a comprehensive planning effort in the Arab world to provide for the labor needed in the petrochemical industry.

202. Nishimura, K. "Manpower Requirements and Development for the New 33-GW Nuclear Generation Plan of Japan." Paper presented at the International Atomic Energy Agency Symposium - Manpower Requirements and Development for Nuclear Programmes, Saclay, 2-6 April, 1979. Vienna: IAEA, 1980. IAEA SM-238/43

> The future planned level of nuclear power generation was recently amended by the Japan Atomic Energy Commission to 33 GW by the year 1985. It means that further construction of at least 19 nuclear power plants of 1000 MW(e) each will be needed for the accomplishment of this new plan during the next seven years. The technical manpower requirement for this new plan is estimated in this paper by use of a typical model, which requires a staff of 100 persons for the normal operation of a 1000-MW(e) nuclear power plant. Among these technical staff members, the number of well-trained and experienced persons, i.e. 'key personnel', is considered to be 28. A comparison between manpower requirement and supply for the new plan is made for reactor operators, technical staff, radiation safety staff and maintenance staff. Through this comparison, nuclear training programmes for the development of manpower needed for operation and maintenance is reviewed both from the aspects of quality and quantity by taking into account the functions of the existing training courses in Japan. In addition, the periodic inspection of a nuclear power plant requires almost 1300 persons per power plant; they do not belong to the nuclear power companies, but to either directly related or subcontracted companies. The educational problems for the 'key personnel' among these people are discussed, and a new programme is proposed. (IAEA)

203. Organization of Arab Petroleum Exporting Countries. "A Preliminary Field Study on the Labor Force in the Oil Sector of the Member Countries," OAPEC Bulletin, 1975. (in Arabic)

> The Arab countries included in the study are: United Arab Emirates, Algeria, Saudi Arabia, Bahrain, Syria, Iraq, Qatar, Kuwait, Libya, and Egypt. The study focuses on the different oil and petrochemical projects and their future needs of labor. It also assesses the training potential in the oil-producing countries.

204. Ostho, John B.   "Occupational and Training Requirements for Expanded Coal Production," Proceedings of the National Conference on Meeting Energy Workforce Needs, Washington, D.C.:   February, 1980. Silver Spring, Maryland: Information Dynamics, Inc., 1980. pp. 67-74.

The share of coal from total energy supply is expected to jump from 20 to 50 percent by 2020.   Coal is relatively labor intensive. Yet, the industry has been plagued by labor productivity decline, by industrial relations problems and by high rates of labor turn- over and absenteeism.   The article tackles the occupational and training requirements for expanded coal production.   The focus is on DOE project and the training survey to determine the extent to which coal mine employers (350 companies) provide training for their employees over and above minimum Federal and state require- ments.   The preliminary findings based on partial returns indicate the recent development of coal industry training programs (both formal and on-the-job training).   The project also develops the occupational requirements for coal mining and the future training requirements.

205. Palabrica, R. J. and Eugenio, M. R. "Manpower Development Programme for the First Nuclear Power Project in a Developing Country – The Philippines Experience." Paper presented at the International Atomic Energy Agency Symposium – Manpower Requirements and Development for Nuclear Programmes, Saclay, 2-6 April, 1979.   Vienna: IAEA,   1980 IAEA-SM-238/44

This paper presents the Philippines experience in training manpower for the country's first nuclear power project.   It traces the history of the Philippine Atomic Energy Commission and its role in the implementation of the project's training programme as a conse- quence of its direct involvement in nuclear science and technology centered in a 1-MW pool-type research and training reactor.   The participation of other agencies, both local and foreign, is also recognized.   A brief exposition of the training courses being conducted by PAEC for middle-management engineers and for the operating staff of the nuclear power plant is presented.   The paper concludes with the guiding philosophy of the Philippine programme, which is to maximize utilization of both local and foreign com- ponents in the training of manpower for the country's first nuclear power project.   (IAEA)

206. Rall, Jane E. Energy-Related Scientists and Engineers: Statistical Profile of New Entrants Into the Work Force, 1976.   Washington D.C.: U.S. Department of Energy, October 1978.   ORAU-147 (NTIS)

The study surveys graduate scientists and engineers between 1973-1975.   About five percent of the surveyed group are involved in energy related work.   The engineers make up two-thirds of the group.   The energy-related graduates work in the same field as their college major and receive higher degrees than the total population.   Females (8.3%) and non-white (2.3% engineers; 1.77% scientist) graduates are underrepresented in energy-related work. Their primary work activity is associated with applied research, design and production as opposed to teaching and management.   The energy-related respondents work for private industry with a higher median salary.

A comparison between the percent graduates and the more experienced workforce is undertaken by major and occupation. It was found that the new entrants majoring in engineering are more involved in energy-related activities than their experienced counterparts. Proportionately more of recent graduates in energy-related work hold masters degrees. More females and less non-whites are onboard. The appendices give the questionnaires used.

207. Richter, Lothar. "Manpower Planning in Developing Countries: New Emphases and Approaches."   Inter-Regional Seminar on Manpower Forecasting and Planning, USSR, October 2-11, 1984.   Geneva: International Labour Office, 1984.

The purpose of this paper is to analyze some of the new emphases on reorientations that have been implemented in manpower planning activities in recent years. Labor market signalling through key informants is discussed. A pluralistic approach is recommended for future involvement in manpower planning. There is increased interest in sectoral manpower planning, specifically in the energy sector. Special attention has been given to the problem of anticipating the requirements of various categories of skilled manpower in order to identify and provide timely inputs into national energy programs. In response to the needs outlined in this report the ILO has initiated a program to assess manpower and training needs. The program's objective is to build up technical capacity in order to assist developing countries in the planning of energy sector manpower.

208. Robeson, John; Barnett, Samuel C.; Wilson, Richard L.; and Ansell, Jim.   "Engineering Students and the Nuclear Industry - the Future?"   Transactions, Vol. 41, March 1982, pp. 40-42.

This article is divided into four mini-articles tackling engineering students and the future of nuclear industry. The idea here is to attract more students into that field. There are great opportunities for collaboration between industry and academia. The utilities should attract both faculty and students to make plants and data an integral part of the classroom curriculum. A review of the future employment opportunities shows that the nuclear power industry needs an estimated 7000 engineering and science graduates during the period 1981-1991. The increase in the nuclear power capability is expected to raise the industry employment from 55,000 positions in 1981 to 71,000 positions in 1991. Market estimates indicate that four to five new nuclear plants a year will start through 1990. Degreed individuals are needed to hold key positions throughout the utility. It is important that the industry attract and maintain the necessary personnel required. It is recommended to introduce "grow-your-own" approach whereby the individual is exposed to and interacts with the field environment.

209. Schiff, Gary S. (editor).   The Energy Education Catalog: Programs in American Colleges and Universities.   New York: Academy for Educational Development, 1981.

This catalog surveys energy programs in higher education. It covered over 500 colleges and universities of all types in all 50

states and District of Columbia. It represents the first comprehensive reference work to include energy education programs and
their descriptions in colleges and universities across the United
States. Both formal and informal programs are included. The
specific types of energy education programs listed cover conventional energy sources, solar energy and other non-traditional forms
(geothermal, wind, biomass). The catalog is cross-indexed by the
name of the institution, by state and by topic. The university
faculty and staff, as well as the student would benefit from such a
publication. Businessmen and government officials, by the same
token, would find the information valuable.

210. Settlemire, Mary Ann. Energy Education Programs: Perspectives for
Community, Junior, and Technical Colleges. Washington, D.C.: American
Association of Community and Junior Colleges, 1981.

This monograph reviews the role of community, junior, and technical
colleges in energy education. It examines the history of energy
use in the United States, reviews the energy legislation, and
summarizes the energy manpower projections for different types of
energy. It describes the approach adopted by the community,
junior, and technical colleges in addressing energy education.
Several forms are noted: facilities conservation, general public
information, short-term specialized courses, certificate and degree
programs. The history of college involvement is short, but their
experiences have been substantial. It outlines, based on a tele-
phone survey of program directors of thirteen colleges, the steps
to be followed (program components) to introduce an energy curriculum into any institution. The monograph also identifies the
possible funding sources for the development and implementation of
energy curricula at post-secondary institutions.

211. Shirley,   Duveen   L.   and   Sweeney,   Deborah   H.   Health
Physics/Radiation Protection Enrollments and Degrees, 1984. Washington
D.C.: U.S. Department of Energy, March 1985. PR-360 (NITS)

The study provides statistical information on enrollment and
degrees for health physics and radiation protection for fall 1984
and includes the trends from 1974 to 1984. It is based on a survey
of 68 institutions. Total enrollment in undergraduate and graduate
programs increased by 13 percent from 1983 to 1984. BA degrees
increased by 7 percent, and MA by 11 percent. The largest employer
of bachelors and doctoral degree graduates was medical facilities
whereas nuclear utilities represented the largest employer for the
masters level. The study also reviews the status of foreign
nationals, women and minorities, as well as, the regional distribution in terms of enrollment and degrees.

212. State of Kuwait. Central Vocational Training Administration.
Council of Ministries. The Labor Force and Training in the Public
Sector, the Joint Sector and the Oil Sector. Kuwait: CVTA, January,
1974. (in Arabic)

The report includes studies prepared by Central Vocational Training
Administration during the year 1973 about the labor force and
training in the public sector, the joint sector and the oil sector.

1. Training in the government sector: professional training
    in the government sector is based on a) organized training
    which is done through the Training Institute and b) on-the-job
    training which is carried under the supervision of technical
    personnel. The training units are categorized into three:
    semi-skilled workers, skilled workers, and technicians.

2. Labor force and training in the joint sector: the study
    includes all the joint sector's companies. Professional
    training in this sector is undertaken through education,
    on-the-job training, organized training, training abroad and
    summer training for the university students.

3. Labor force and training in the oil sector: The government
    shows great interest in the training of labor in the oil
    companies. It encourages young Kuwaitis to join the oil
    sector and to offer them the best opportunities for training.

213. Stoltenberg, Kristian. "Training Philosophy and Strategy in the
Petroleum Industries, as a Consequence of the Impact of Technological
Changes." Paper presented at the Third Arab Energy Conference- Energy
and Cooperation, May 4-9, 1985. Safat, Kuwait: OAPEC, 1985.

The double challenge of mastering advanced technology and supplying
trained and experienced manpower must be faced by any country
experiencing the application of new technology or the development
of new industry. This is especially true within the energy and
petroleum related industries. In the planning stages for basic and
higher technical training, modern training philosophy and methods
should be applied to ensure efficient, systematic and cost
effective training. Close contact is necessary between the
individual plants and the training institutions because detailed
training plans and programs, to be efficient, must be formulated on
the basis of need. Teachers should be retrained or upgraded in the
latest and most efficient training methods. Also special management training programs are necessary in order to ensure the availability of qualified management personnel.

The requirements for successful implementation are 1) clearly
stated objectives, 2) defined roles and responsibilities, 3) established procedures and 4) scheduled actions. The experience of
Norwegian authorities is given in the context of the North Sea
discoveries.

214. Sweeney, Deborah H.; Garey, Robert B.; and Shirley, Duveen, L.
Nuclear Engineering Enrollments and Degrees, 1982. Washington, D.C.:
U.S. Department of Energy, Office of Energy Research, May 1983.
DOE/ER-0165

This report presents data on the number of students enrolled and
degrees awarded in academic year 1981-82 from the 72 U.S. institutions offering degree programs in nuclear engineering or nuclear
options within other engineering fields. The objective is to chart
the changes in the supply of new nuclear engineers in order to meet
the increasing demand for trained personnel to work in this field
given that there has been negligible growth in the number of BA and

MA degrees and a drop in the doctoral degrees awarded in the late seventies.   The report also offers historical data regarding enrollment degrees and placement of graduates as well as regional distribution.   It also tackles female, minorities and foreign nationals participation in nuclear engineering degree programs. (ORAU)

215. Sweeney, Deborah H. and Shirley, Duveen L. Nuclear Enrollment and Degrees, 1983. Washington, DC: U.S. Department of Energy, Office of Energy Research, May 1984. DOE/ER-0165/1

This report presents data on the number of students enrolled in the Fall of 1983 and the degrees awarded in academic year 1982-83 from 75 U.S. institutions offering degree programs in nuclear engineering or in other engineering disciplines with a nuclear option sufficient to equip graduates to function as nuclear engineers.

The report includes historical survey data for the last decade and provides information such as trends by degree level and program option, foreign national student participation, female and minority student participation, and placement of graduates. Also included is a listing of the universities by type of program and number of students. (ORAU)

216. Sweeney, Deborah H. and Shirley, Duveen L. Nuclear Engineering Enrollment and Degrees, 1984. Washington, D.C.: U.S. Department of Energy, Office of Energy Research, March 1985. DOE/ER-0165/2

This report presents data on the number of students enrolled and degrees awarded in academic year 1983-84 from 71 U.S. institutions offering degree programs in nuclear engineering and nuclear options within other engineering fields.

The report includes historical survey data for the last decade and provides information such as trends by degree level and program option, foreign national student participation, female and minority student participation, and placement of graduates. Also included is a listing of the universities by type of program and number of students.

217. Taha, Hussein. "Technology Transfer to the Arab Hydrocarbon Industries." Paper presented at the Third Arab Energy Conference - Energy and Cooperation, May 4-9, 1985, Algiers, Algeria. Safat, Kuwait: OAPEC, 1985.

This paper discusses the importance of new technology for the Arab hydrocarbon industries, the need for the technology transfer and the difference between transferring and copying technology.   It describes the forms of technology acquisition, the diffusion and control of technology, as well as the sources, problems and costs of transferring technologies in a variety of areas.   The paper also emphasizes that technology transfer is dependent on the training of personnel on a new technologies and the suitability of technology for local conditions.   Proposals to improve technology transfers are offered.

218. Taylor, Robert P. Decentralized Renewable Energy Development in China - The State of the Art. Washington, D.C.: The International Bank for Reconstruction and Development - The World Bank, 1982.

This report describes China's decentralized renewable energy mass-based development system. It reviews its activities in the areas of biogas, small hydroplants, forestry, solar energy and wind energy. It also evaluates the Chinese approach as implemented during the seventies. China achieved remarkable success in the first two areas. China is working towards achieving self reliance. One central aspect to that concept is local participation in development through the operation of local units. This perceived as an effective measure in relation to rural development. The approach emphasized highly applied research, the development and diffusion of intermediate technology and the strengthening of local technological capabilities and the training of low-level technicians among the workers and the training of low-level technicians among the workers and the peasants. The process of technology diffusion in China's rural areas involved local adoptive R&D training extension. This was in accordance with the science policy of the Cultural Revolution. The strength of the system is in its ability to popularize technology based on local funds, labor and resources and its adaptation to local conditions. The problems included poor technical performance and low quality as well as ineffective management in many local projects. There was also a lack of attention to regional and national planning and coordination. China is now still focusing on the local level, but efforts are directed toward greater emphasis on fundamental research, better planning, more effective training of the local people and assistance to local units.

219. Tendler, Judith. Electric Power in Brazil: Entrepreneurship in the Publis Sector. Cambridge, Massachusetts: Harvard University Press, 1968.

The power industry was divided between private and public enterprise. This has been important to relieve the problems and power supply in Brazil's south central region. Distribution which is "operation-intensive" suited the foreign utility and its conservative approach to expansion-generation, which is "construction-intensive", suited the new state enterprises. The rash of hydro-generation drew vigorous talent to the power sector and commanded a surprisingly impressive performance from the new state managers. They liked generation because of the uninspectability of the activity and its technology-intensive nature protected them from the interference of the states that sponsor it. Generation is a highly specialized activity in comparison to distribution. Its working force is smaller, more highly skilled and homogenous.

The separation of public and private enterprise and overemphasis on generation did not necessarily perpetuate problems of rate stalemate and distribution neglect. It just initiated the sequence by which these problems are eventually resolved. This success illustrates the general thesis that the technologies vary as to their political vulnerability, their ability to draw out and train

competent talent and their capacity to face politically
antagonistic institutions.

220. Texas A & M University.   Center for Career Development and
Occupational Preparation.   Energy-Related Careers.   Washington, D.C.:
U.S. Department of Health Education and Welfare, 1978.   ED167414 (ERIC)

This booklet outlines the career opportunities referenced as
"OCUPACS" in the field of energy. The objective here is to assist
high school students to understand the opportunities available in
the effective utilization and conservation of energy resources.
The careers are grouped into three categories: manufacturing,
business and industry, and electrical energy production.   The
fields covered in the first grouping include: R and D, process,
plant operation, plant, and environmental control engineer. The
second grouping presents the architect in energy, management in
energy business, technical communication, and how to start a small
business in energy. In the third grouping, twelve occupations are
reviewed and include: organic chemist, chemical engineer, petroleum engineer, petroleum geologist, exploration geophysicist,
exploration geochemist, mining engineer, mining geologist, nuclear
engineer, industrial health engineer, radiation protection engineer, and nuclear physicist.

221. UNCTAD Secretariat.   "A Framework for Policies to Strengthen the
Technological Capacity of Developing Countries in the Energy Sector," in
Pradip K. Ghosh (editor).   Energy Policy and Third World Development.
Westport, Connecticut: Greenwood Press, 1984, pp. 180-191.

The rate of growth of energy consumption in the developed countries
has outpaced their domestic energy production. In fact, the energy
consumed today in the US and Europe for transportation (private)
alone matches the total energy consumption of the developing world.
A few developing countries export energy supplies. The majority of
the developing countries depend heavily on external supplies of
commercial energy.

Technological considerations in the energy sector assumes greater
importance because of the size of the investments involved. They
have been high in the third world and will increase considerably in
the future. Developing countries face several constraints in
attempting to meet the technological aspects of energy investments
with their own capabilities. They lack the necessary skilled
manpower. The scarcity of engineering and managerial skills
further complicates the problem. Although the equipment for energy
projects is largely imported, efforts towards the manufacture of
energy capital goods are underway. The mere size of energy investments, their impact on the economy and the role of the public
sector in their implementation provide challenging opportunities to
reduce technological dependence in the energy sector. To strength-
en their technological capacity, they need to: 1) Plan the
training of skilled manpower. This is an area in which prospects
for regional and international cooperation are promising. This
needs to be complemented with the development of engineering and
management expertise. 2) Improve conditions for transfer of energy
technologies. 3) Accelerate the transfer for surveying, exploring

and developing primary energy sources. 4) Reorient purchase policies of public utilities. 5) Promote research and development activities. 6) Manufacture energy capital goods. All these issues are interrelated and effective in bringing a desired change over a period of time.

222. UNCTAD Secretariat. "Issues in Transfer and Development of Energy Technology in Developing Countries," in Pradip K. Ghosh (editor). Energy Policy and Third World Development. Westport, Connecticut: Greenwood Press, 1984. pp. 168-177.

This article examines the concerns and issues of the growing energy sector in developing countries. During 1976 these countries spent 14.4 billion on capital and exploration projects in the petroleum industry. Forty four percent of this investment went to production activities, followed by transportation and refining. They require highly skilled manpower. Most developing countries are experiencing a shortage among nationals and must rely on foreign personnel from industrialized countries to manage the energy sector. Many developing countries are attempting to educate their population in the two disciplines that are closely linked to the energy sector, natural science and engineering. In addition, skilled technicians and operations are needed for the development of the energy sector. Skill formation for the energy sector is carried out in their training institutes as well as in many specific transfer of technology agreements.

223. U.S. Department of Education. Energy and Education Action Center. Proceedings of the National Conference on Meeting Energy Workforce Needs, Washington, D.C., February, 1980. Silver Spring, Maryland: Information Dynamics, Inc., 1980.

The theme of the National Conference on Meeting Energy Workforce Needs is to examine the availability of trained manpower to implement energy programmes in the 1980's. The focus is on education and training capabilities to meet such needs. The evaluation of the future workforce requirements in energy producing industries (solar, coal, nuclear power, and renewable energy) is given in order to assess the different energy education/training programs, including vocational, adult education, and career education. Other aspects include the opportunities for minorities and women as well as linkages between industry and education to ensure the optimum use of education and training resources.

224. U.S. Department of Energy. Energy-Related Manpower, 1982. Oak Ridge, Tennessee: Oak Ridge Associated Universities, December 1982. DE83005418 (NTIS)

Manpower implications of shifting trends in energy R and D and production are examined. The analysis relies heavily on projections of energy production and of federal funding for energy R and D from the US Department of Energy's Energy Information Administration, the Office of Management and Budget, and the National Science Foundation. Estimates of private funding for energy research and development were derived from projections by the National Science Foundation and the McGraw-Hill Economics Department. Although negligible through 1983, in the rest of the decade energy-related employment is likely to grow in almost every engineering and scientific field. One way to gauge the likely adequacy of the future supply of labor is to compare the expected growth over the second half of this decade with the level of new degree awards at present by comparing the relative degree rankings for Ph.D. fields. This simplified approach points out areas where projections of growth indicate the greatest likelihood of shortage in the event that degree awards do not increase, i.e., mining, petroleum, and chemical engineering. A similar approach was used to assess the adequacy of supply of B.S./M.S.-level scientists and engineers for five fields especially important to energy. For most of these fields a comparison of expected growth with the current level of degree awards suggests that enrollments and degrees will be adequate during the 1980s without substantial increases beyond current levels. Even in petroleum engineering, where projected growth outstrips the current level of B.S. degree awards, there may be little need to increase awards over the present levels. (ORAU)

225. U.S. Department of Energy. Energy-Related Manpower, 1984. Oak Ridge, Tennessee: Oak Ridge Associated Universities, January 1985. DE85008120/XAB (NTIS)

Overall energy sector employment growth in the 1980s will be considerably less than previously projected, owing to increased conservation, depressed oil prices and increased reliance on market-oriented solutions, and a shifting Federal role in energy R and D. Although the overall rate of energy-related employment growth is expected to be low over the next 5 years, the increasingly technical nature of energy-related work combined with the high proportion of scientists and engineers in the energy segment results in substantial growth in expected demand in a number of science, engineering, and technical occupations. Because many of these occupations are also critically needed in the economy in general, the energy sector will be competing in an already tight labor market. The supply of new graduates appears to be a current problem in some fields. Lower enrollments and, hence, a lower number of graduates appear to be constraints on the labor supply at all degree levels in health physics and nuclear engineering. Low enrollments are occurring in all Ph.D. fields where faculty is a supply constraint in some engineering fields. Foreign nationals who obtain degrees in US remain to work in the US are an additional supply source of employees. Energy R and D funding is expected to continue to shift from public to private sources, reducing demand for Ph.D. scientists and engineers while increasing demand for specialists at the BS/MS level in energy-related R and D work. (NTIS)

226. U.S. Department of Energy. Directorate of Energy Research. Division of High Energy Physics. Report of the Subpanel on High Energy Physics Manpower of the High Energy Physics Advisory Panel. Washington, D.C.: U.S. Department of Energy, June 1978. DOE/ER-0010 UC-34 (NTIS)

This report examines the production of new researchers in high energy physics and their holding of permanent positions for the period 1972/3 - 1976/77. The number of new Ph.D. graduates in high energy physics has decreased in recent years from 278 to 137. There is a balance between the number of Ph.D.s in experimental and theoretical high energy physics. There is a total of 1716 Ph.D.s in this field. They are employed by 78 universities and 5 national laboratories. About 92 percent hold tenured positions with a higher proportion of experimentalists (62.5%) relative to theorists. The remainder held Research Associate, Assistant Professor or laboratory equivalent appointments. Given the age distribution of the tenured persons, retirements will be small during the next decade. The promotion pattern at the universities averaged 90 persons per year, equally distributed between experimentalists and theorists. The national laboratories promote 5-6 experimentalists per year and just one fourth of that number for theorists. It is important to reveal all the career opportunities available in the field. It is recommended that a temporary program be created to retain additional number of experimentalists and theorists in semi-permanent positions until retirements become significant.

227. U. S. Department of Energy. Office of Intergovernmental Affairs. Energy - Related Doctoral Scientists and Engineers in the United States, 1977. Washington D.C.: U.S. Government Printing Office, April 1980.

This report provides information regarding the number and charac- teristics of doctoral level engineers and scientists in energy- related activities. This information is offered in an effort to indicate actions necessary to ensure that adequate numbers of these scientists and engineers are available when needed to aid in the development of the nation's energy resources and technologies (R & D).

This 1977 survey concluded that approximately 10 percent of the 284,000 doctoral scientists and engineers employed in the United States spent a significant proportion of their professional time on the topic of energy and fuel. Forty-seven percent of these scien- tists and engineers worked in business or industry and 38 percent worked in educational institutions. A comparison of the 1975 and 1977 surveys showed that the proportions of all doctoral energy- related scientists and engineers rose from 7.9 to 10 percent.

228. U. S. Department of Energy. Office of Energy Research. Manpower Assessment Program. Doctoral Scientists and Engineers Working in Energy-Related Activities, 1981. Washington, D.C.: U.S. Department of Energy, April 1983. DOE/ER-0127/1

The study focuses on the doctoral scientists and engineers who devote most of their professional time to energy or fuel-related activities. The data is based on a 1981 survey sponsored by the Office of Energy Research in the U.S. Department of Energy (DOE), by the National Science Foundation (NSF) and by other federal agencies. The study examines 1) trends by employment field, 2) trends by energy source, 3) mobility between degree and employment fields, 4) type of employer, energy source paid work activity, 5) U.S. Government funding, and 6) demographic characteristics. A small increase in the total number of doctoral scientists and engineers working in energy-related activities was reported between

1979 and 1981. But, there was a notable shift in the sectors of
employment in favor of the private sector reflecting a decline in R
& D federal expenditures and an increase in industrial expenditures. There was no growth in the number of PhDs from educational
institutions between 1979-1981. The future implications of PhD
supply and demand trends are assessed in light of the proposed
reduction in overall federal funding for energy R & D through 1984.
The net reductions in employment demand would affect various fields
of science and engineering differently. During the second half of
the decade, federal funding for energy R & D is projected to rise.
In those fields where demand would exceed supply, employers would
attract candidates from other disciplines by offering higher
salaries and benefits as well as rely on foreign nationals who
completed their education in the U.S.

9. U.S. Department of Housing and Urban Development.   Solar
monstration Program. "Installing Solar: Training Expands to Meet the
ed," HUD Solar Status, September 1978. Washington, D.C.: GPO, 1978.
D-PDR-189-11

This article focuses on the installation and maintenance training
currently available throughout the nation. The study outlines the
two-year solar programs, short courses, home study, and installation aids. Solar training courses offered by vocational schools
differ by number, duration and coverage. Finally, colleges,
universities and vocational-technical schools that offer solar
installation programs are listed.

230. U.S. Department of Labor and U.S. Environmental Protection Agency.
Environmental Protection Careers Guidebook. Washington, D.C.: DOL,
1980.

The guidebook provides descriptions of the activities, responsibilities, and educational and training requirements of the major
occupations directly related to environmental protection.   Of
special importance is the section on radiation control.   This
section undertakes to review the appropriate legislative acts, the
employment opportunities, the specific occupations with its job
requirements. The nuclear energy field has a high concentration of
engineers, scientists, and technicians constituting about 50
percent of the nuclear power workforce. Opportunities for employment depends on the building of nuclear plants. National growth
projections reflect a declining trend. The occupations for emergency services radiation coordinator, health physicist, radiation
laboratory technician radiation monitor, radiation protection
engineer, radiation protection specialist, and radiological
instrument technician are reviewed. A list of Federal job
information centers is provided. The appendices offer information
on the sources of financial aid and the postsecondary environmental
education programs by state and type of pollution.

231. U.S. House of Representatives. Domestic Energy Resources - Parts 1
and 2. Hearings Before the Subcommittee on Elementary, Secondary and
Vocational Education and on Employment Opportunities of the Committee on
Education and Labor, May 24, June 5 and 26, 1979. Washington D.C.:
GPO, 1979.

The Hearings in two parts were done before the Subcommittee on Employment Opportunities and the Subcommittee on Elementary, Secondary, and Vocational Education. They relate to the assessment of manpower needs and training programs in relation to domestic energy development. The hearings focus on the need to develop synfuels industry including the introduction of appropriate manpower training programs for the unskilled and unemployed persons to familiarize them with the industry operations. There is a definite need for skilled manpower for synfuels plant construction and operation. The historical background of synfuels development is given with recommendations for legislative and financial support to stimulate the industry. Federal assistance and loan guarantees with incentive measures are recommended. DOE should undertake appropriate actions to encourage synfuel commercialization. It is also recommended to set up a federal corporation to produce or assist in the production of synfuel. The case of the Republic of South Africa synthetic petroleum coal conversion program is offered.

232. Weidlich, H. H. "How to Use and Develop a Limited Quantity of Qualified Manpower with a Maximum Gain in Safety." Paper presented at the International Atomic Energy Agency Symposium – "Manpower Requirements and Development for Nuclear Programmes," Saclay, 2-6 April, 1979. Vienna: IAEA, 1980. IAEA-SM-238/11

Starting with IAEA investigations into manpower requirements for nuclear installations the paper defines those jobs which implant safety during planning, construction and operation. The necessary numbers of experienced people for these jobs are derived. As practically measurable safety work goals and relevant manpower costs are given, optimum safety-oriented manpower strategies are clearly shown. The strategies can be applied by nuclear importing and exporting countries. (IAEA)

233. Williams, Milton A. "Initiating, Organizing, and Managing Energy Management Programs," in W.C. Turner (editor). Energy Management Handbook, New York: John Wiley and Sons, 1982.

A sound comprehensive energy management program is very important for energy savings. First top management must be dedicated and committed to an energy conservation program. This chapter outlines a detailed plan of action that could apply to large and small companies. It is a result-oriented program. The organizational set up as well as the primary functions of a manager – planning, leading, controlling, promoting, and monitoring – are fully documented.

234. Woods, Jacqueline E. Profiles in Energy. Washington, D.C.: National Council for Resource Development, August 1980.

The publication provides an overview of the major steps necessary to engage in planning for the energy education process. It focuses on the two-year post-secondary institutions and their efforts to incorporate energy-related activities and services into the educational offerings. Steps to systematic program planning at the local level are outlined in terms of 1) availability of natural energy resources, 2) types of training needs, 3) anticipated jobs

available after training, and 4) the addition of new programs or
upgrading of existing ones to include energy-related components in
the curricula.   A summary of major employment, educational and
training impact of the National Energy Act is provided by type of
activity.   Furthermore, a sampling of energy programs by type of
activity is provided to demonstrate innovations that could be
adaptable to other educational settings.

235. The World Bank. Mobilizing Renewable Energy Technology in
Developing Countries: Strengthening Local Capabilities and Research.
Washington, D.C.: The World Bank, 1984.

This report discusses the renewable energy technology in the
developing countries in terms of 1) assessment of needs for
building local expertise to adopt such technology and review of the
status of national capability and the scope of existing aid programmes, 2) the need for research and evaluation of extensive
list of technologies appropriate to such economies, and 3) the
institutional arrangements for their implementation. Awareness of
the potential importance of renewable energy technology differs
among countries. The report categorizes three levels: a) fully
committed and with a full range of technical skills; b) commitment
but with limited capability; and c) minimal policy commitment and a
low level of capability. There is a definite need for conducting a
training program for professionals. At the national level, the
formulation of policies on renewable energy is necessary.

The paper reviews the production and use of biomass from primary
energy and its potential. Biomass represents an important primary
energy source for developing nations. Research efforts need to
focus on this area. The paper recommends a country-by-country
approach to assess need for enhancement of national technical
capabilities through international assistance. Different types of
programmes are needed for biomass production and other technologies
for the use of direct solar, wind, etc. The undertaking of such
programs requires the capitalization on national and regional
institutions already in existence. Small teams of high-level
manpower would be required.

6
Women in Energy

236. Marcus, Gail H. "The Status of Women in the Nuclear Industry," Bulletin of Atomic Scientists, 32, April 1976, pp. 34-39.

This article investigates whether sex discrimination exists in nuclear-related job areas. The American Nuclear Society (ANS) surveyed a group of men and women. The questionnaires were broken down into three parts: 1) personal information, 2) employment history, 3) present employment and relevant details. The response rate was relatively high (45% for women and 29% for men). The results indicate, despite the limitations of small sample size, statistical significance. Women were relatively underrepresented in direct nuclear engineering training (28% compared to 41% of the men). Part-time employment of women outnumber that of men (6:1 ratio). More women than men have been unemployed (2:1 ratio), underemployed (3:1 ratio) or non-technically employed (2.4:1 ratio). Twenty percent attribute such labor underutilization to sex discrimination. Women were underrepresented in the upper salary and management scales. The overall salary differences were too large to reflect differences in human capital factors alone (i.e. background or experience). The employers' distribution reflects women overrepresentation in federal government and underrepresentation at utilities or universities. In conclusion, there is definite grounds for discrimination against women in nuclear-related professions. It is particularly apparent in the case of older women. Many women are denied fellowship/jobs because it is believed that their labor market attachment is intermittent. Further improvements in the nuclear field are yet to be made in the years to come.

237. Random, Mary Lou. "Opportunities for Women in Energy," Proceedings of the National Conference on Meeting Energy Workforce Needs, Washington, D.C., February 1980. Silver Spring, Maryland: Information Dynamics, Inc., 1980, pp. 327-333.

The problem for women in the energy sector is very similar to that of women in the economy as a whole or the problem of employment and wage discrimination. Women make up only 6.7 percent of the energy-related occupations. Only 2.9 percent of women doctorates are working in energy-related fields. The article stresses the need for education and training opportunities to allow many women currently engaged in the energy industry to more promising jobs. Women represent an important human resource pool that needs to be tapped especially in the event of labor shortages.   There are incentives for unions, educational institutions and employers to recruit women.   Efforts to increase opportunities for women in energy need to be made at the local level.

7
A Union Perspective

238. Baratz, Morton S. <u>The Union and the Coal Industry</u>. New Haven, Connecticut: Yale University Press, 1955; reprint ed., Port Washington, New York: Hennikat Press, 1972.

This work appraises the effect of the policies of the United Mine Workers (UMW) in the bituminous coal industry in the perspective of the economy as a whole from the 1930's to 1950's. More specifically, it discusses how union wage policy has affected the structure and behavior of the industry and therefore, the supply and demand for labor. This book shows that when union policy attempted to eliminate regional wage differentials to prevent disastrous interregional competition, the southern mines were transformed to high-cost operations. Because of this the southern mines experienced large gains in employment that were offset by declines in the northern mines. Therefore, between 1935 and 1948, overall employment in the industry rose only slightly. No positive case can be made for or against unionism on economic grounds. Efforts to control union activities must be directed instead against the political effects of unions.

239. Cameron, John and Wood, George. "Energy Organizing in the 1980's," <u>Socialist Review</u>, No. 52, July-August, 1980, pp. 120-129.

This article presents the problems and possibilities of organizing around energy issues through a coalition structure. Many of these efforts have been initiated and led by socialists united around anti-corporate energy issues. Yet, many obstacles need still to be overcome if the potential of this activity is to be realized. The successful efforts of the Central Illinois Consumer Energy Council (CICEC) are discussed. Their programmatic task centers on questions of control of energy production, the need for alternative energy sources and the immediate problems low-income and working people face under the current system of energy production. The socialists role in the larger energy movement is one of initiating serious coalition work, bringing in the grass roots, developing a short and long-term socialist program for energy in the U.S. and seeing coalitions as leading to new political formations.

240.   Kurchak,   John.   "Solar   Energy: One   Union's   Viewpoint,"
Alternatives: Perspectives on Society and Environment, Summer 1978, pp.
14-16.

Workers in the construction industry support the further
development of nuclear energy.   A major nuclear energy project
amounts to ten years of work for a large number of workers.   The
article argues in favor of solar energy as a clean source of
renewable energy for the future.   The Sheet Metal Workers' Union
has been actively promoting energy conservation several years
because it can provide work for the unemployed sheet metal workers.
There is a lacking federal commitment in Canada to promote
conservation measures.   The American experience shows the future is
already here.   Research and development funding for renewable
energy resources are estimated at 3 percent compared to 75 percent
for nuclear energy.   Some steps have been taken in the right
direction but they do not go far enough.   There is a gap of
knowledge as union workers do not fully understand the impact of
the new technology in terms of jobs and the country's energy needs.
The response of a survey of 21 unions or federations in Canada on
the role of solar home heating was very disappointing.   Only one
trade union replied.   Solar energy has exciting prospects for the
future.   Future jobs depend on how fast it is implemented.   Several
recommendations were made to that effect including more publicity,
more research, more cooperation with interested groups, and more
government involvement and funding.

241. Oil, Chemical and Atomic Workers International Union.   OCAW Energy
Policy. Denver, Colorado: OCAW, May 10, 1977.

The oil, gas and nuclear industries employ more than 70,000 members
of Oil, Chemical and Atomic Workers International Union (OCAW) in
the U.S.   In addition, there are over 100,000 OCAW members associated with chemical and allied products industries.

The future of energy affects the future of these workers.   This
study is undertaken by OCAW and calls for: 1) Extending permanently
the crude oil entitlements program under the Energy Policy and
Conservation Act of 1975.   The two alternatives proposed of complete deregulation of crude oil and a new system of equalization of
taxes are not favorable to the interests of the American people.
The first would disrupt the economy and trigger substantial wind-
falls to oil producers.   The second would be administratively
cumbersome.   2) Promotion of domestic refining of imported crude
oil as opposed to the importation of refined products.
3) Legislation mandating prompt and complete disclosure of information dealing with energy.   4) Non-support of vertical divestiture
of the petroleum industry.   5) Opposition of natural gas deregulation.   6) Measures towards energy conservation.

242. Solar Energy Research Institute.   Market Development Branch.
Organized Labor and Solar Energy. Golden, Colorado: Solar Energy
Research Institute, February 1979. SERI/TR-62-148

This report discusses the role and implications of organized
labor's involvement in the developing of solar technologies.   The

project covered 18 international unions. The focus of the efforts by
the Solar Energy Research Institute (SERI) has been communication. The
labor community will play a significant role in the production,
distribution, installation, and maintenance of solar technology. Union
leadership is aware of the need for the reduction of dependence on
fossil fuels and on the role of solar energy technology in terms of job
creation and solution to energy crisis. Communication was maintained
through interviews with union leaders, sponsoring of a national
workshop, the identification of labor programs and policies (through
surveys and regional conferences etc.) The findings reveal the absence
of jurisdictional disputes. Only the Sheet Metal Workers had
sophisticated training programs which emphasize the skills needed for
solar installation. All of the unions agree that the needed training of
their members for work in solar technology would require a very minor
adjustment to present training programs. Most of the union leaders
interviewed lacked information on the costs, benefits, obstacles and
employment prospects for solar energy. They wanted full involvement and
a close relationship with SERI. The report includes a summary of the
National Labor Leadership Workshop in Solar Technology held in June
1978. (SERI)

8
Future Energy Options and their Employment Implications

243. Anderson, Marion and Parisi, Carl. American Jobs from Alcohol Fuel. Lansing, Michigan: Employment Research Associates, n.d.

This report discusses the economic implications of producing fuel alcohol (ethanol) to replace imported oil. The technology and feedstocks for producing alcohol fuel from biomass are currently available. It is estimated that investing $12 billion between 1981-1986 to build plants capable of producing 6 billion gallons of fuel alcohol yearly would have a high employment generation potential. A total of 960,000 new jobs would be created. About 409,000 jobs would be generated in construction (160,000) indus- trial (210,000) and service (39,000) jobs. An addition 71,000 jobs would be needed for the operation and maintenance of the plants of which 31,800 represent the personnel for plant operations, and over 39,000 jobs will be with the supporting services. Five direct jobs per million gallons of alcohol produced is calculated. The secondary employment (through the multiplier) to be generated from the spending of the workers directly related to the industry is estimated to be 480,000 jobs.

The plants do not require initial high investment and their distribution is expected to be throughout the nation. There is no trade-off between food and fuel and the world supply of needed food will not be reduced. The production of fuel alcohol would allevi- ate the energy problem, guarantee employment and help the economy prosper.

244. Bell, S.E. and Little, J.R. Biomass Energy Systems: Descriptions and Employment Requirements for Typical Operations. Washington, D.C.: U.S. Department of Energy, Office Of Conservation and Renewable Energy, September 1981.

Several energy biomass systems are described. Of particular interest are the employment requirements of the operations of the processes involving the direct combustion of wood, specifically wood chip harvesting and transportation, wood-fired industrial boiler systems, and wood-fired utility power plants. In the wood chip harvesting sector exact labor requirements and productivity depend on the type of operation. Staffing for a typical selecting cutting, whole tree operation involves 8 to 10 workers. Clear-cutting, generally, involves one less worker but output remains the same.

The operation of a wood-fired industrial boiler system of any size will generate full employment for at least one person per shift because constant surveillance is required. The larger boilers may require 16-24 boiler operators and maintenance employees, 19.4 truck drivers to deliver wood chips and 54.5 woodchip harvesters.

In wood-fired utility power plants, around-the-clock supervision involves 16-25 people for a 10MW plant, 30 to 40 people for a 25MW plant and 40 to 60 people for a 50MW plant. Outside employment could involve up to 27.1 transportation and 76.2 wood harvesting employees. No modern wood-burning electric power plants have been built so the temporary construction employment requirements are difficult to ascertain.

245. Brauer, Dieter. "Fuel from Alcohol: Blessings and Curses of a New Technology," Development and Cooperation, January/February, 1980, pp. 11-13.

The Brazilian experience is illustrated with the development of a new energy alternative, ethyl alcohol. Also known as ethanol, this product is made from sugar cane. The Brazilian government became devoted to its production in an effort to decrease the country's dependence on oil imports, where 85 percent of requirements were imported. The government program provided large subsidies to the construction of sugar refineries but not to the sugar cane production. In fact, the government held the purchase price lower than the costs of production. As a result, the smaller farms were reducing labor and paying them starvation wages. Most of the sugar workers could only find any type of work and income during six months out of the year.

On the other hand, in Southern Brazil, where the country is more developed, the mechanized farmer experienced large profits. As a result, the entrepreneurs bought up more land. Ultimately, the situation led to small farmers being driven out of business and the production of foodstuff neglected. In Brazil, the workers were unable to buy the ethanol in which their government had produced for their use. Clearly, the price of maintaining the auto industry (as a consumer society luxury) is at the expense of small farmers in the rural areas. Although the government is still "proalcohol", the disadvantages of a mono-culture are obvious. The economic and social implications of the programs are serious. The program "fuel from the farm" most certainly will be a dead end.

246. Bungay, Henry R. Energy: The Biomass Options. New York: John Wiley & Sons, Inc., 1981.

The continuing deficits due to oil imports and the redistribution of wealth among nations is a threat to the U.S. economy. The prices of fertilizer, plastics, fabrics and many other items have risen due to the combination of petrochemicals plus energy. These rising prices cause sales to decline and production to decrease

leading to fewer jobs. Cheaper forms of energy are needed to prevent massive unemployment.

This book describes in detail the many biomass options that can be available through increased research and development efforts. The author contends that within the next 20 to 30 years, biomass fuels can replace fossil fuels and petrochemicals. As this transformation takes place, new companies and opportunities for investment will emerge, creating new jobs.

247. "Business & Economy: Five Energy and Employment Facts," Michigan Energy Journal, Vol. 7, No. 3, Summer 1983.

The article documents the findings of studies on energy conservation and renewable energy and their positive effects on employment. First, the installation of 2.2 million residential solar heating units by 1985 would generate 58,000 jobs and save millions of barrels of oil. Second, approximately 200,000 jobs per year would be created if energy conservation and efficiency standards are met by year 2000. The production and installation of solar hot water and space heaters reflecting the national goal of 20 percent solar could create an additional 400,000 jobs per year. Third, the adoption of a federal home weatherization program would provide for a minimum of 50,000 jobs per year with a fifth to two-thirds saving of fuel consumption to low-income households. Fourth, energy conservation in residential and commercial buildings would lead to a net employment gain of 350,000 jobs in 1990 and 900 million barrels of oil equivalent saved annually by that year. Fifth, the introduction of a comprehensive energy conservation/-solar program in all sectors of the economy would generate 2.2 million direct jobs plus millions of additional indirect jobs. All these jobs would be distributed across the nation and would help the unemployed. All skill levels would be represented, both unionized and non-unionized.

248. California Public Policy Center. Jobs from the Sun, Employment Development in the California Solar Energy Industry. Los Angeles: California Public Policy Center, 1978.

A scenario for solar energy and the California economy is provided. It shows that solar energy means jobs and economic growth. The responses of 45 percent of the solar firms in California showed that feasible uses of solar heating between 1981 and 1990 could generate 1) over 375,000 jobs per year, 2) $4.2 billion in increased personal income, 3) $15.1 billion in increased Gross State Product, 4) $19.8 billion in tax savings, and 5) $10.2 billion in exported capital savings. Additionally, the state's unemployment rate of 7.8 percent will be cut in half by 1977 with the generation of these new jobs. The two areas with the greatest structural weaknesses, manufacturing and construction, will benefit greatly from the solar industry development.

249. Centre for Alternative Industrial and Technological Systems. Oil and Petrochemicals Industry - The Threats to Jobs in the UK. London: CAITS, The Polytechnic of North London, September 1982.

The oil and petrochemical companies are looking outside Europe for future expansion and investment thanks to government taxation and monetary policies. This international relocation will negatively impact jobs. The reduction of capacity (25-30%) implies the loss of 90,000 jobs over the next few years. The report reviews the role of 1) the British government, 2) EEC, 3) U.S., and 4) OPEC in relation to this issue. The report also closely examines the operation of large multinational corporations as the Royal Dutch/Shell and British Petroleum (BP). Company wide solidarity is recommended to contain the power of management through multiunion, multi-plant organizations. Effective union coordination will fight to preserve the jobs and the industry as a whole. To rely on the action of a sympathetic government will not be of much help.

250. D'Alessandro, Bill. "Employment: Bright Hopes and Base Realities," Solar Age, Vol. 8, No. 7, July 1983, pp. 19-20.

The article discusses the employment prospects of the solar industry. It reviews the findings of the Solar Work Survey in California in terms of occupational groupings, salaries and job tenure. The average salary in the industry is reported to be $17,500. Presidents and owners of typical business engaged in installation are paid between $28,000 to $35,000. It also presents information on the sales representatives in wholesale and retail operations. The average term of employment is three years. Recruitment is mostly done by word-of-mouth and newspaper advertising. Prior solar experience is desirable but not required. The industry is described as quite competitive and quoting the director of solar division of Solcoor Inc., it is maintained that "one in ten entrepreneurs can make it."

251. Dauth, Jurgen. "Fuel from Thailand's Agriculture," Development and Cooperation, January/February, 1980, p. 13.

Thailand will reduce its dependence on oil by producing alcohol from biomass. The land is available due to a slowly growing population. The government, at present, spends $1.2 billion annually for the production of gasohol. It plans to increase its annual production of agricultural raw material, as sugar cane, cassava and sorghum. The planned alcohol factories will act as built-in stabilizers to the fluctuating export prices. In essence, agricultural production for fuel is not competing with food production. It is estimated that small farmers get to gain annually from the gasohol program. The program is being implemented.

252. DeGrasse, Robert; Bernstein, Alan; McFadden, David; Schutt, Randy; Shiras, Natalie; and Street, Emerson. Creating Solar Jobs: Options for Military Workers and Communities. Mountain View, California: Mid-Peninsula Conversion Project, Nov. 1978.

This study assesses how military workers and communities can utilize their skills to develop solar energy. Solar energy, as a renewable resource, can promote energy self-sufficiency and expand job opportunities through community growth. Government spending for solar energy development will create more jobs than comparable expenditures in military production. Four solar technologies are

examined (active and passive space heat, photovoltaics, and wind turbine generators) in terms of market conditions, skills and number of jobs. Active solar heaters are expensive. They are expected to create 100,000 jobs in California in the next decade (i.e. exceeding the employment generation of other energy sources). The passive solar heating industry costs less but faces institutional barriers. Jobs generated include technicians and engineers. The last two technologies need still further developments to bring their costs down. It appears that transfer of workers could be accomplished with minimum or no training. Only the engineers and managers would require major reorientation. It appears that large corporations will dominate the solar industry. Coalition programs are needed to challenge corporate control. Government incentives and policies would have a definite impact on the speed of solar energy development and its structure.

253. Elliot, D.A. Energy Options and Employment. London, England: Centre for Alternative Industrial and Technological Systems, March 1979.

Market criteria, such as the number of jobs created, are used to make decisions regarding possible energy investment options for energy supply technology. Specifically, an estimation of the number and types of jobs to be created by a United Kingdom investment programme geared toward conservation and renewable energy alternatives is compared to the jobs likely to be created by a nuclear programme that is currently being considered. The results indicate that the nuclear programme, assuming a 40 GW capacity is achieved, is estimated to create 660,000 person years of direct and indirect work through the year 2000, at a cost of approximately 35,000m pounds. Assuming only 25GW is put into operation, 400,000 person years is estimated. In comparison, a moderate non-nuclear conservation programme that exploits renewable sources and which will provide the same energy capacity as the nuclear proposal, will create approximately 1,520,000 person years through 2000. Breakdowns by technology, industry and skill of the 'alternative' programme are presented.

254. Elliot, David. "Energy and Jobs," Energy Manager, April 1979, pp. 23-25.

This article examines the employment prospects of future energy policies. Energy has the highest capital employed per capita of any industry. The Center for Alternative Industrial and Technological Systems (CAITS) in the UK undertook a study to estimate the total number of direct and indirect jobs that would be created by a non-nuclear alternative energy/conservation programme. The findings indicated that the diversion of investment funds from nuclear to conservation and alternative energy programmes would result in the same level energy with the additional creation of one million more job-years of direct and indirect work. The CAITS non-nuclear programme encompasses investments in energy conservation (building insulation), domestic and industrial heat pumps, and various renewable alternatives (solar, wind, wave, tidal). Jobs would be created in many of the areas of the industry and of the country (e.g. 150,000 job-years in building construction, and 60,000 job-years in power engineering). CAITS is also noting that alternative programmes are appealing to trade unionists. More employment analysis is needed for the UK. The study emphasizes the need for the development of new skill intensive renovation, repair and recycling industries in the form of small and decentralized enterprises. The recycling of drink containers was estimated to create 117,000 new jobs. Selective use of automation is required. The key question is to achieve a balance between capital and labor, reflected in the choice of technology.

255. Gallagher, J. Michael; Carasso, Meir; Baramy, Ronald; and Zimmerman, Ralph G. Direct Requirements of Capital, Manpower, Materials and Equipment for Selected Energy Futures. San Francisco, California: Bechtel Corporation, 1976.

This report summarizes an analysis of the direct capital, manpower, material and equipment requirements needed to implement candidate energy futures provided by the Energy Research and Administration (ERDA). The analysis is based on an application of the Energy Supply Planning Model developed by Bechtel Corporation for the National Science foundation. The objective of the study is to calculate direct resource requirements for the construction and operation of facilities. Two cases are considered: the limited imports and the free imports. The comparison of their manpower categories indicates that for construction manpower requirements:

°   1976–85 average annual requirements for engineers decreased by 3% to 59,000 man-years/year.

°   1976–85 average annual requirements for craftsmen increase by 3% to 276,000 man-years/year.

°   Peak requirements decline for craftsmen and engineers

°   Average annual requirements increase for chemical, petroleum and operating engineers, pipefitters, electricians and boiler-makers while decrease for civil, mining and nuclear engineers.

For operations resource requirements the comparison indicates that:

°   1976–85 average annual requirements for engineers and craftsmen are essentially unchanged.

°   Nuclear and mining engineers, equipment operators and under-ground miners decrease by 0%–10%.

The operations resource impacts are less pronounced than the difference between free imports case and limited imports case construction requirements.

256. Gimbel, Liza and Drucker, Charles. "The Shadow on Solar Jobs "Soft Energy Notes, Vol. 3, No. 6, December/January 1981, pp. 28–31.

There are wide variations in the estimates of new employment by solar industries. One conservative calculation reports 4 million person-years of employment would be needed by year 2000. But, federal policies influence the distribution of solar employment

through the programs and incentives encouraging new energy technologies.   The present program promotes solar installations in
middle and upper income homes at the expense of lower income ones.
The high-tech solar not only creates fewer inner-city solar jobs
but also generates fewer semi-skilled and unskilled positions.   If
employment is to reach low-income groups, innovative financing, job
training and community organization programs are needed.   The
Citizens Energy Project calls for such measures.   The article
criticizes federal and state agencies and labor unions in not
supporting this trend.

257. Goldemberg, Jose.   "Renewable Energy Sources: The Case of Brazil,"
Natural Resources Forum, No. 3, April 1979, pp. 253-262.

The modernization of Brazil has resulted in increased energy
consumption per capita.   Brazil pays about $4 billion per year for
oil imports which presented severe problems to the development of
its energy.   The Brazilian government has actively supported the
development of alternative energy sources.   The expected energy
profile for 1990 looks unacceptable as petroleum share will
increase to 46 percent.   The article reviews the future energy
situation.   It is reported that hydropower, nuclear for electricity
supply, and biomass production of liquid and gaseous fuels could
play a very important role in alleviating the energy situation
(energy autonomy scenario).   It will be necessary to double the
amount of investment in energy production.   Economically, it seems
possible that Brazil has shown that it has the political will and
the technological expertise necessary to redirect its energy
consumption patterns away from the dependence on imported oil.

258. Grossman, Richard and Daneker, Gail.   Guide to Jobs and Energy.
Washington, D.C.:   EFFE, 1977.

The Environmentalists for Full Employment (EFFE) believe that
energy systems such as nuclear fission and fusion, conversion of
coal and shale to gas and oil and expanded coal-fueled electric
generation are too destructive.   This publication provides support
for the EFFE's recommendation to use solar energy as an alternative.   They contend that solar energy combined increased energy
efficiency will actually lead to a more stable economy and more
jobs than the larger systems.

259. Gutmanis, I.; Guiland, L. Stephen; McBrayer, Rita A.; and Paul,
Arthur.   Study of Manpower Requirements by Occupation for Alternative
Technologies in the Energy-Related Industries, United States, 1970 to
1990 Vol I.   Washington, D.C: National Planning Association, August
1974.   PB-243 474 (NTIS)

The objective of the study is the estimation of the future manpower
requirements for energy construction operations and maintenance as
well as design and R & D.   Two different scenarios are considered
for the years 1975-1990.   The projections are to be made under the
same prevailing circumstances and for accelerated development.
Manpower coefficients were developed for all occupations in the
energy sub-sectors.   They are expressed in man-years per unit of

output or per dollar outlay which were projected into the future
based on an anticipated energy output. The accelerated program
means more energy output or dollar outlay per year and hence more
manpower. A numbering system was devised for the energy
sub-sectors allowing for lower-level classification. The DOL
manpower occupational categories for operation and maintenance
activities and construction were adopted. The industries covered
in the study include petroleum, gas, nuclear, synthetic fuels,
shale oil, geothermal, solar, transportation, and facilities. The
actual projections of manpower requirements in the energy sectors
through 1990 are presented in tables at the end of the report.

260. Hannon, Bruce M. "Energy, Labor and the Conserver Society,"
Technology Review, Vol. 79, March/April 1977, pp. 47-53.

The emphasis is on how a society determined to conserve energy
could increase economic stability, employment and equity. Such a
conserver society should forecast scarcity and plan for shortages
of energy. In general, the conserver society would experience
increase use of labor and capital associated with the decreased use
of energy.

The conservers must fully assess the labor impacts of the energy
conservation plan. Using the energy and employment impact model of
the Energy Research Group at the University of Illinois Center for
Advanced Computation, the job potential per unit of energy saved
(quadrillion B.T.Us.) for each conservation project is estimated.
In terms of strategies, it is argued that the shift to lower energy
use could be achieved by establishing priorities and operating on
an activity-by-activity basis or by imposing a tax on energy whose
return could be used to encourage full employment. Another
alternative is the use of energy rationing.

261. Hoffman, Kurt. "Alternative Energy Technologies and Third World
Rural Energy Needs: A Case of Emerging Technological Dependence,"
Development and Change, Vol. 11, July 1980, pp. 335-365.

The developing countries are more and more conscious of the role of
renewable energy resources to satisfy their future energy requirements, particularly their rural energy needs. They have launched
major R and D efforts in this direction. These countries are
well-endowed with renewable energy resources, particularly solar,
wind and biomass. Furthermore, because alternative energy systems
have the potential to be small-scale and low-cost, they are most
appropriate to rural areas which suffer the most severe energy
shortages. Since the early 1970s, however, interest for alternative energy technologies has spread so widely in the advance
industrial countries that they are the subject of major public and
private investment efforts. The Third World is considered as a
potential market. In the international context, aid agencies are
earmarking funds for projects in this area.

The implications for the developing countries are clear: renewed
technological dependency. The developing countries experience a
relative disadvantage in this area. In addition to their
relatively low levels of R & D, they are constrained by their

limited technical skills. Yet, the importation of Western renewable energy systems would deny the development of local capabilities. To implement the renewable energy policies, however, will involve trade-offs in the short run which can be costly in terms of finance and welfare. The social costs of investing in capability development will be high for a long period of time (i.e. fewer rural people will have adequate access to energy supplies). The issue of technological capability reflecting the set of required skills that developing countries must acquire to generate an indigenous solution to their usual energy problems is a highly complex one. The developing countries should keep a close eye on the technological developments in the West which would require additional evaluative capabilities. Finally, their energy strategy should fit with the overall policies for agricultural development and employment creation.

262. Khan, A.R. and El-Difrawi, A.   "Capital, Manpower and Training Requirements For Selected Projects on Non-Oil Sources of Energy," OAPEC Review, Vol. VI, No. 2, Summer 1982, pp. 161-172.

This paper attempts to project the capital, manpower and training requirements for the development of non-conventional sources of energy by year 2000. Selected alternative energy sources are examined, specifically fossil fuel (coal, oil shale) and solar projects within the context of the U.S. economy. Estimates of capital investments, in the absence of commercial installments on marketed processes, cannot be exactly defined and are presented within maximum and minimum limits. Much larger investments are needed relative to conventional sources of energy. It was also found out that the average capital cost of solar is at least two or three times that of fossil fuel. Manpower requirements are determined in number of person-hours for all skills required. Occupational skills are not all that different from those of a typical industry. However, specialized training is needed for mining operatives, process operators in the case of fossil fuel projects in the use of modern equipment and new conversion technologies, and for engineers in solar technology.

263. Koshaim, Bakr H.   "Solar Program Activities at the Saudi Arabian National Center for Science and Technology (SANCST)," OAPEC Bulletin, Vol. 12, No. 4, April 1986, pp. 18-27.

This paper describes the activities carried out at the Saudi Arabian National Center for Science and Technology (SANCST), including joint programs with the U.S. and West Germany. The first joint program is called SOLERAS and is intended to achieve cooperation in solar energy technology. The major research projects include: urban, rural and industrial solar applications, photovoltaic power system, solar controlled environment agriculture, and solar thermal research. The resource development activities include the establishment of high technology laboratories for advanced solar research and the training of personnel to develop educational programs and sponsor basic research. The objective of the joint program with the Federal Republic of Germany is to develop means of generating electricity using high energy conversion systems and to undertake solar hydrogen production and utilization (HYSOLAR). The project covers personnel exchange and educational program.

264. Laitner, Skip. "Energy, Jobs and the Economy," Solar Age, Vol. 2, No. 9, September 1977, pp. 14-16.

This article advocates the use of solar energy and conservation techniques as a viable energy alternative. The author states that the correlation between GNP and energy consumption suggested by business and energy leaders does not hold. Citing a three-year study by the Ford Foundation, it is shown that a less energy intensive economy would slightly increase employment over existing levels of energy consumption. In fact, real GNP would be approximately twice as large. A comparison of job intensities and costs of solar electric and nuclear sources in the year 2000 is given. The calculation results show that solar technologies will provide approximately four times more jobs than nuclear technologies at a lower cost. The skills and training required for solar projects are less demanding than nuclear so more people qualify for employment. Also, solar technologies provide on-site generation which allows work to be closer to home. Both of these facts mean that a wider variety of people can actually work on the installations.

265. Laitner, Skip. "The Impact of Solar and Conservation Technologies Upon Labor Demand." Paper presented to the Conference on Energy Efficiency, May 20-21, 1976. Washington, D.C.: Public Citizen's Critical Mass Energy Project, May 1976.

This study examines the employment potential of conservation and solar options and compares it to the nuclear alternative. It is maintained that the adaptation to a less energy intensive economy will yield a higher employment level over the existing use levels of energy consumption. At a 2 percent energy growth rate (below 3.5 percent historical annual growth rate) the U.S. would by year 2000 generate 1.5 percent more jobs and use 37.7 percent less energy. In Europe, higher per capita incomes are associated with half of the U.S. energy use per person. A comparison of the manpower requirements for the construction of a 1000 megawatt electrical nuclear and coal power plant reveals that the latter will result in 40 percent higher labor requirements. A growing number of scientists and legislators are turning to the solar option to sustain the economy. At the average price of oil of $11 per barrel by year 2000, about 30 percent of energy needs could be satisfied by the sun. A comparison of different solar technologies with nuclear technology reveals that 2.5 times more jobs per unit of energy are associated with the first alternative. In addition, the transition to a decentralized solar program can greatly help the unemployed and the disadvantaged persons. Unfortunately, solar technology did not receive the attention it deserves. It is strongly recommended that the federal government mandates its adoption in the federal buildings. The success of this legislation and program depends on the full support of consumer groups and unions.

266. Mason, Bert and Armington, Keith. Direct Labor Requirements for Select Solar Energy Technologies: A Review and Synthesis.   Golden, Colorado: SERI, August 1978.   SERI/RR-53-045

Labor and manpower implications of solar energy adoption are potentially important because the application of solar energy technologies would create expanded job opportunities.   It is important to have qualified and well-trained manpower to manufacture, design and install solar equipment.   All the existing research on solar job requirements focuses on liquid flat-plate collectors for residential space heating (SH) and domestic hot water (DHW) heating.   The results of three separate studies on direct job requirements for SH and DHW are presented.   The comparison reveals considerable variance in their estimates because of differences in purpose, approach and level of detail.   Additional research is warranted particularly in relation to other types of solar energy technology, 2) learning effects incorporation, 3) the manpower requirements of ancillary components necessary to complete solar systems, 4) the indirect and displacement effects of solar technology diffusion, and 5) types and geographic dispersion of jobs created by the solar industry.

Labor costs represent almost one-half of total direct costs.   For combined DHW/SH the labor cost component represents one-quarter to one-third of total system cost.   To determine total job requirements for design, manufacture, installation and maintenance of residential solar systems, market penetration projection is used on the basis of three different studies.   There is a wide range of estimates of solar job potential.

267. Niblock, Tim and Lawless, Richard. "Prospects for the World Oil Industry," Proceedings of a Symposium on the Energy Economy. Durham, England 1-10, May 1984. Co-sponsored by the Petroleum Information Committee of the Arab Gulf States and the University of Durham, England. Dover, New Hampshire: Croom Helm, 1985.

This symposium on the prospects for the world oil industry tackles four different topics.   The first topic discusses the prediction of strategic reserves.   It outlines the geological factors that are critical to the prediction of hydrocarbon potential and examines the distribution of present proven reserves and future discoveries. While two-thirds of the world's oil resource has been found, 60 percent of the world's gas has been found but only 15 percent has been produced.   Most new oil will be discovered in areas currently being explored.   More capital and more manpower will be needed towards this goal.   The second topic is about industrialization in the Arab States of the Gulf.   It emphasizes the need towards a comprehensive framework whereby alternatives need to be carefully planned.   It is stressed that the industrialization scheme would extend beyond the oil era.   The third topic is on scenario planning in the context of energy development as it relates to Shell Oil Company.   It focuses on the fact that scenario planning is not extensively used by Shell and could be of very great help to meet the uncertainties surrounding the energy world.   The scenarios would reflect on the energy demand changes for the next two decades.   The fourth topic discusses national income accounting and petroleum with a case study on the Arab Gulf Cooperation Council Members (AGCC). The article establishes a relationship between wealth and income and estimates the income generated from the proceeds of petroleum exports of five of the AGCC members.

268. Petersen, H.C. "Estimation of Sector Sales and Employment Changes Associated with Solar Space and Water Heating Development," Solar Energy, Vol. 22, No. 2, 1979, pp. 175-182.

There is little available information on sector-specific sales and employment impacts of a large-scale solar space and water heating industry. This study identifies those sectors of the economy which would be most affected by increased solar utilization and estimates the magnitude of the changes. The basic methodology involves augmenting an existing Input/Output table to include sectors reflecting solar technology. Data required to augment the matrix were obtained from questionnaires returned by existing firms involved in collector manufacture or solar space and water heating system sales. The augmented I/O matrix is inverted to generate a direct and indirect requirements matrix. The elements of this matrix estimate the changes in total sector output resulting from changes in final demand of other sectors. Estimates of final demand for solar heating systems by 1985 and projections of annual energy savings associated with solar installations to that time were obtained from existing studies. Using the computed direct and indirect requirements matrix and the assumed changes in the composition of final demand estimates of changes in sales and employment were made for 131 sectors of the U.S. economy. It was determined that the sectors most affected by solar development will be those involved in electricity generation and the mining, refining, and fabrication of metals, especially copper. The proportionate changes in industry sales and employment are not expected to be very great. Only copper rolling and drawing is changed by as much as two percent. This finding suggests that the U.S. economy can accommodate an expanded use of solar heating without undue stress. (PPL)

269. Scales, John K. and Popkin, James M. Energy and Jobs: Employment Implications of Alternate Energy Development and Conservation Strategies in the North East. Washington, D.C.: Coalition of Northeastern Governors' Policy Research Center, March 1983.

The objective of the study is to highlight the job impacts of the increased development and utilization of alternative energy and conservation strategies in the Northeast. The report focuses on energy dependence and unemployment and the inability of the region to develop its own energy sources. The paper reviews the economic effects of resulting energy transfer payments in terms of unemployment, low tax revenues, reduction of social and public services flight of industries, and declining personal income. But, the region does have the potential for the development of alternative energies (solar, wood, wind power, coal), and conservation. The consequent employment potential is significant. The study presents the substantial resources available and their possible employment effects for the eight states of the North East region. Solar development could create 40,000 jobs by year 2010. Cogeneration and distinct heating would offer 2,000 jobs. The results would be positive by stabilizing energy prices, and increase the area's disposable income. To materialize, a full commitment is required at the regional and state levels to provide for the high capital requirements and long-term planning. Different organizational options are considered ranging from a regional energy corporation to a joint-industry-government conference. In addition, employment, training and information system would focus on energy resource development. Financing measures (e.g. grants, tax benefits) are also needed to stimulate the development of alternative energy sources and conservation. The report outlines the barriers facing the development of each alternate energy resource and recommends policies to remove such obstacles. Private sector initiatives should be encouraged and need to complement regional and state policies.

270. Schachter, Meg. The Job Creation Potential of Solar and Conservation: A Critical Evaluation. Washington, D.C.: U.S. Department of Energy, November 26, 1978.

Solar proponents assert that a solar and conservation-oriented economy will generate more employment than conventional or nuclear energy alternatives. Although the employment effects of alternative energy systems have not been determined with accuracy, the study indicates a very highly favorable effect on direct job creation. The study presents a conceptual framework for analysis to compare quantitative and qualitative aspects of job creation among energy alternatives. Upon the review of the state-of-the-art, several findings are reported. First, solar energy generates 55-80 times more direct jobs than Liquefied Natural Gas (LNG) for the same amount of energy; whereas conservation measures would add 26 times more direct jobs. Second, solar heating systems add 2 to 8 times more direct jobs than conventional power plants for the same amount of energy. Finally, conservation measures are more economical (cost/job) than nuclear power but will generate less direct jobs than nuclear and other conventional power plants at energy equivalent. It is recommended to adopt a policy of combining solar and conservation measures maximizing direct job creation at lower total costs.

271. Schiflett, Mary and Zuckerman, John V. "Who Will Be Working in Solar Energy Jobs?" Solar Engineering Magazine, Vol. 4, No. 5, May 1979, pp. 13-16.

It is expected that solar industry will expand by the late 1980s. Its labor force is anticipated to reach 50,000. Union involvement has been remote and not supportive. It is expected, however, that every job in solar energy will add to the total number of jobs in the nation. The implementation of new solar technology will open up new activities in insulation, piping, sheet metal, etc. Solar jobs would be evenly distributed throughout the nation. It offers opportunities for high skills in advanced research. Long periods of special training will not be required. In fact, solar energy creates two to eight times as many direct jobs as conventional power plants. A study by Council on Economic Priorities (CEP) concludes that a solar/conservation strategy option would create

270 percent more direct employment with huge energy saving than a nuclear option at a lower cost.

272. Simeone, R. N. and Hodgkinson, I. A. "The Prospective United Kingdom Nuclear Energy Programme Up to 2000 AD and the UKAEA's Role and Manpower Requirements." Paper presented at the International Atomic Energy Agency Symposium - Manpower Requirements and Development for Nuclear Programmes, Saclay, 2-6 April, 1979, Vienna: IAEA, 1980. IAEA-SM-238/17

This paper begins by surveying the development of the United Kingdom nuclear industry, its organization in both the public and private sectors of the economy, and changes in the numbers employed up to the present. The possible future nuclear programme and overall manpower needs, and the UKAEA's role and manpower requirements within this programme, are outlined. Manpower problems arising from national shortages of engineers and technicians, reviews of arrangements for their education and training, and also from the pattern of historical development of the UKAEA, are described. UKAEA arrangements for formulating and implementing personnel policies, current policies for recruitment, carrier management and in-service training and their relationship to present and future needs are then discussed. The final section draws attention to UKAEA facilities for the training of staff from other organizations in the United Kingdom and from overseas.

273. Stahel, Walter R. and Reday-Mulvey, G. Jobs for Tomorrow: The Potential for Substituting Manpower for Energy. New York: Vantage Press, 1981.

The feasibility of the labor-for-energy substitution is presented in relation to EEC member countries. The findings are valid for the United States. Labor could be substituted for energy in different ways. Three approaches are identified: 1) Reversal of energy-labor substitution trend in sectors where mechanization has increased the number of unattractive jobs or caused job dequalification, 2) Recycling, and 3) The restucturing of industrial production processes through the introduction of new reconditioning loops in the life-cycles of industrial materials on products which will replace the traditional linear production-use disposal patterns. These methods offer the greatest potential for the creation of new and satisfying jobs with higher degrees of skill and to achieve a substantial reduction in energy consumption. Two case studies in the context of the French economy are presented from the automobile and construction industries. Economic growth and energy-labor substitution in that country will represent the overall evolution in the European Community. Between 1965-1969 the number of skilled workers increased by less than 7 percent while the number of unskilled workers grew by 60 percent indicating the spreading of less attractive repetitive jobs in the auto industry. This has increased turnover and absenteeism and resulted in resorting to immigrant workers. By the same token, the construction industry employs approximately 50 percent more foreign workers than the average industry.

The selection of the most appropriate approach depends on the sectors under consideration. The reconditioning approach is recommended for the auto industry. The example of the long-life cars (20 years) is described. The manufacturing of such cars combined with a thorough periodic sensitive-parts replacement and programmed reconditioning would result in substantial energy and material savings creating a sizeable increase in employment in "reconditioning" workshops. Finally, there are institutional barriers (vocational, educational, industrial, and consumer behavior) to the substitution of manpower for energy which could be overcome by changes in education or legislation or by a new industrial strategy.

274. Texas A&M University. "Cooperative Study Assessing the Need for Solar Technicians," Texas Energy and Mineral Resources, Vol. 4, No. 1, November/December, 1977, p. 1.

This article discusses the assessment of the need for trained manpower in the solar energy industry. It is very expensive to install a solar unit. Hence, there is a need for trained workers to increase the reliability of the operation and to reduce its costs. The article references a study undertaken by a team of researchers at Texas A&M University. The project tasks are handled by three separate groups: an equipment group, a market penetration group and a task analysis group. The findings would reveal the required numbers of people to be involved in solar installation and maintenance as well as the corresponding necessary level of training. The availability of such a manpower pool will positively impact the commercialization of solar technology.

275. United Nations Economic Commission for Western Asia. Arab Energy: Prospects to 2000. New York: McGraw-Hill, Inc. 1982.

This publication projects the Arab world's energy configuration to year 2000. Projections for solid fuels, natural gas and primary and conventional thermal electricity are made based on the evaluation of existing programmes and perspectives of countries of the Arab World. The projections are carried out in the framework of a regional energy balance model. Oil will continue to play a very important role for the region. At present, the Arab world provides about 60 percent of total world crude oil exports. The development of alternative energy sources will still not make substantial contributions to the Arab energy balance before the turn of the century. Energy conservation becomes one of the primary concerns of an Arab country's long-term crude-oil production policy. This requires an accurate assessment of Arab recoverable resources. It was estimated that aggregate reserves to production (R/P) ratio of 20 to 1 would be reached by year 2009. It is argued that the building of export refineries, as planned by many Arab countries, present difficulties in terms of capital intensity, long gestation period and high proportion of skilled and professional workers. They should be so designed to meet the Arab demands for refined products. The operation of reconstituted crude oil, however, would be particularly profitable in the Arab world. It is projected that the Arab world's total primary energy requirements (TER) are expected to increase by 8.7 percent a year until year 2000. The contribution of natural gas to TER is expected to rise. The share of primary electricity is expected to pick up. The rapid development of nuclear power would contribute significantly. The projections are presented in million toe (M toe), in million barrels per day of oil equivalent (M boe/d), and in exajoules (EJ). As to the contribution of individual countries to total energy exports, Saudi Arabia, Iraq and Algeria would dominate. The study also examines the future world demand for energy and for oil. It points out that the world supply and demand situation in 1990 is not that serious for total primary energy as it is for oil where a global deficit is anticipated (3 to 11 percent of world demand).

276. United Nations Economic Commission for Western Asia. New Renewable Energy in the Arab World. Baghdad, Iraq: UNECWA, 1981.

The study examines the development of new and renewable energy alternatives in the Arab World. Key indicators as source of energy, supply availability and energy needs should determine the extent of their utilization. This study analyzes such sources as geothermal heat, biomass energy and energy produced by wing power in terms of feasibility and potential use in the Arab World. Finally, the adoption of an integrated Arab regional strategy for the development of new and renewable sources of energy is strongly recommended.

277. U.S. Congress. Subcommittee on Energy of the Joint Economic Committee. Employment Impact of the Solar Transition. Washington, D.C.: GPO, 1979.

Using the energy projections prepared by the Data Resources, Inc. for 1977-90, the study estimates the impact on employment of the introduction of energy conservation and solar energy measures. The Bureau of Labor Statistics maintains that the growing consumption of energy is not accompanied by a corresponding rise in employment in the energy industry or industries which use energy. The new jobs in the energy industry are related to the expansion of electricity production. These jobs would require large scale migration. This is referred to as "the business as usual" scenario. This is contrasted with an active program of conservation and renewable energy (CARE) on a national level. CARE strategy covers residential and commercial, industrial, transportation use and portable fuels, as well as, electricity production. The energy savings and the number of jobs generated by these measures depend on the magnitude of the investment. The projections distinguish between direct (1,120,000) and indirect (1,050,000) jobs. Energy savings would reduce employment (1,137,000 fewer jobs) in the fuel-producing and electric generating industries, but the saved funds can be spent to purchase additional goods and services leading to an additional 1,870,000 jobs created. A total of 2,903,000 jobs would be created. These jobs are characterized by being widely allocated throughout the economy.

278. Victor, Peter A.; Hathaway, George; and Lubek, Jack. Solar Heating and Employment in Canada. Toronto, Canada: Middleton Associates, 1979.

The development of a solar heating industry will help alleviate the unemployment problem of Canada. It will also provide a stimulus to the manufacturing sector of the economy. It is important to solicit the support of the government and the private sector to this end. Possible contributions of solar technology to energy supply and employment must be carefully assessed. This study examines the overall employment impacts of solar industry in Canada. Seven heating systems are described and estimates of direct labor requirements are provided. An employment impact simulation model is developed to examine the employment and energy implications of different assumptions about the future of solar heating. The model allows for the aggregation of the five regional areas. The results projected to year 2000 indicate 1) direct employment amounting to 170,000 man years with 50 percent concentration in construction labor and engineering services; 2) indirect employment estimated at higher than the triple of direct employment; 3) the regional rates of implementation determine the employment distribution (direct and indirect) throughout the nation; and 4) small off shore oil employment displacement.

279. Watson, A.L., and Zimmerman, Ralph G.J. Projected Annual Resource Requirements at the National and Regional Level for the Department of Commerce Energy Forecast 1985 and 2000. Prepared by Bechtel National, Inc. Springfield, Virginia: National Technical Information Service, March 1979. PB80-126956 (NTIS)

This report describes the resource implications at the national and regional level for a "likely" energy supply and consumption forecast for 1985 and 2000 by the Department of Commerce. Total energy resource consumption is projected by Commerce to increase at an average annual rate of 1.8 percent for the 1977-2000 period. Electric energy consumption is projected to grow at 4.2 percent per year. U.S. energy consumption, expressed in quadrillion Btu's (quads) is projected at 87 quads in 1985 and 116 quads in the year 2000.

Projected energy supply and consumption levels from the Department of Commerce were simulated using the Energy Supply Planning Model, which calculated the direct resource requirements for capital, labor, materials and equipment, land and water, and operations and maintenance costs to construct, operate, and maintain energy-related facilities at the national and regional level.

Results of the analysis indicate the largest capital requirements by energy sector are for electric power generation facilities (53 percent), coal-fired power plants in particular. Total annual energy-related capital requirements are projected to grow at an average rate of 2.6 percent per year during the forecast period, from an annual level of $50 billion in 1977 to about $87 billion by 2000. Labor requirements increase at an even higher rate of 3.2 percent, with the largest increase, in relative terms, for manual skills, suggesting a move toward more labor-intensive forms of energy supply. Both capital and labor requirements are projected to move from Western to Eastern regions - in the year 2000. This reflects the projected decline in oil and gas production, coupled with the more rapid increase in electric energy consumption in the more heavily populated Eastern regions. Such a trend could have a favorable impact on the economic outlook of the industrialized regions in the Eastern United States. (NTIS)

280. The World Bank. Alcohol Production from Biomass in the Developing Countries. Washington, D.C.: The World Bank, September 1980.

Biomass ethanol can be produced from sugars, starches, and celluloses. Its technology could be easily transferred to most developing countries. It requires medium-size units and could be easily located in the rural areas and would provide employment to the rural people. This paper discusses the potential and prospects of ethanol production from biomass in the developing countries. Ethanol is an organic chemical with different applications. The economics of alcohol production and consumption depends on the performance of the agriculture, industry, and energy sectors of individual countries. It can be used as a boiler fuel and would substitute for fuel oil. It can be used as gasoline substitute taking advantage of its physical and chemical characteristics. Moreover, it could substitute diesel and could also be incorporated in different chemical applications. The historical ethanol consumption is reviewed for the U.S., the European Economic Community, Japan, India, and Brazil. Prices of ethanol greatly differ among major consuming countries. The developing countries with surplus agricultural production and energy deficiency are the likely candidates to adopt an ethanol program. It is estimated that the jobs potential is high. In Brazil, for instance, an additional employment of 45,000 is estimated for 1980-85 at an investment cost of U.S. $10,000 per job created. Close coordination among the petroleum, industry, and agriculture sectors. This could be accomplished towards developing a comprehensive national alcohol program. World Bank can provide good assistance to the individual countries.

APPENDICES:
Country Classification

Geographic Regions

North America
Canada   44, 23, 102, 240, 278
United States   5, 6, 7, 10, 11,
       13, 16, 17, 19, 20, 21, 24,
       26, 27, 29, 30, 34, 37, 38,
       39, 41, 42, 43, 44, 45, 46,
       47, 48, 49, 50, 52, 54, 56,
       57, 58, 59, 60, 61, 64, 65,
       68, 69, 70, 71, 73, 74, 75,
       76, 77, 78, 79, 81, 82, 83,
       84, 85, 86, 87, 88, 90, 93,
       94, 95, 96, 97, 98, 99, 100,
       101, 103, 104, 105, 106, 108,
       109, 110, 111, 112, 113, 115,
       116, 118, 120, 121, 122, 123,
       124, 125, 126, 127, 128, 132,
       134, 135, 140, 141, 142, 143,
       144, 145, 146, 149, 151, 153,
       154, 156, 157, 162, 172, 173,
       174, 175, 179, 180, 181, 184,
       185, 186, 188, 190, 191, 196,
       199, 200, 204, 206, 208, 209,
       210, 211, 214, 215, 216, 220,
       223, 224, 225, 226, 227, 228,
       229, 230, 231, 233, 234, 236,
       237, 238, 239, 240, 241, 242,
       243, 244, 246, 247, 248, 250,
       252, 255, 256, 258, 259, 260,
       261, 263, 264, 265, 266, 268,
       269, 270, 271, 273, 274, 277,
       279, 280

Oceania
Australia   35

Income Groups

DEVELOPING COUNTRIES

Low Income

Oil importers
 Bangladesh
 Ghana
 India
 Pakistan
 Sri Lanka

Oil exporters
 China

Middle Income

Oil importers
 Argentina
 Bolivia
 Brazil
 Chile
 Colombia
 Greece
 Kenya
 Korea, Republic of
 Lebanon
 Philippines
 Singapore
 South Africa
 Taiwan
 Thailand
 Turkey
 Uruguay

Oil exporters
 Algeria
 Ecuador
 Egypt
 Iran
 Iraq
 Mexico
 Nigeria
 Oman
 Peru
 Syrian Arab Republic
 Trinidad and Tobago
 Tunisia
 Venezuela

INDUSTRIAL MARKET ECONOMIES
 Australia
 Canada
 France
 Germany, Federal Republic of
 Italy

 Japan
 Norway
 Spain
 United Kingdom
 United States

HIGH INCOME OIL EXPORTERS
    Bahrain
    Kuwait
    Libya

Qatar
Saudi Arabia
United Arab Emirates

CENTRALLY PLANNED ECONOMIES
    German, Democratic Republic
    USSR

SOURCE: The World Bank. <u>The Energy Transition in Developing Countries</u>
(Washington, D.C.: The World Bank, 1983), pp. XIV-XV.

U.S. Regions

Directory of Publishers

Alternatives: Perspectives on
Society and Environment
Trent University
Peterborough, Ontario
K9J 7B8 Canada

Alyson Publications
40 Plynpton Street
Boston, MA 02118

American Association of
   Community and Junior Colleges
One DuPont Circle, N.W.
Washington, D.C. 20005

American Society for Engineering
   Education
11 DuPont Circle
Washington, D.C. 20036

Arab Labor Organization
c/o Arab Information Center
747 Third Avenue
New York, NY 10017

Arab Petroleum Training Institute
Baghdad, Iraq

Argonne National Library
9700 S. Cass Avenue
Argonne, IL 60439

Bechtel Corporation
Post Office Box 3965
San Francisco, CA 94119

Brick House Publishing Co., Inc.
3 Main Street
Andover, MS 01810

CEPAL Review
United Nations Economic
   Commission for Latin America
Casilla 179-D
Santiago, Chile

Centre for Arab Unity Studies
Beirut, Lebanon

Coalition of Nuclear Governor's
   Policy Research Center, Inc.
400 North Capital Street,
Suite 282
Washington, D.C. 20001

Colorado Department of Labor
Denver, Colorado

Contractors Mutual Association
1101 - 15th Street, N.W.
Washington, D.C. 20005

Council of Economic Priorities
84 Fifth Avenue
New York, NY 10011

Croom Helm
51 Washington Street
Dover, New Hampshire

D. C. Heath Company
125 Spring Street
Lexington, MA   02173

Development and Change
Sage Publications Limited
28 Banner Street
London EC1Y 8QE England

Development and Cooperation
German Foundation for
   International Development
Hans-Boeckler - Str. 5
5300 Bonn 3, W. Germany

Energy
Pergamon Press, Inc.
Maxwell House, Fairview Park
Elmsford, NY   10523

Energy Economics
Butterworth Scientific Limited
Post Office Box 63
Westbury House, Bury Street
Guildford, Surrey GU2 5BH England

Energy Policy
Butterworth Scientific Limited
Post Office Box 63
Westbury House, Bury Street
Guildford, Surrey GU2 5BH England

Environmentalists for Full
   Employment
1101 Vermont Avenue, N.W., Room 305
Washington, D.C.   20005

Finance and Development
International Monetary Fund
Publications Unit
700 19th Street, N.W.
Washington, D.C.   20431

Government Printing Office (GPO)
Superintendent of Documents
710 North Capital Street, N.W.
Washington, D.C.   20402

Gower Publishing Company
Old Post Road
Brookfield, Vermont   05036

Greenwood Press
88 Post Road, West
Post Office Box 5007
Westport, CT   06881

Information Dynamics
11 Claybrook Drive
Silver Springs, Maryland   20802

International Atomic Energy Agency
Wagramerstrasse 5
Post Office Box 100
A-1400 Vienna, Austria

International Bank for
   Reconstruction and Development
   The World Bank
1818 H Street, N.W.
Washington, D.C.   20433

Institute for Economic Research
University of California at
   Los Angeles
Los Angeles, CA   90024

Institute of Applied Manpower
   Research
Indraprastha Estate
Ring Road
New Delhi, India   110002

International Human Resources
   Development Corporation
Boston, Massachusetts

International Labor Organization
CH-1211 Geneva 22, Switzerland

International Scholarly
   Book Service
Post Office Box 1632
Beaverton, OR   97075

The Institute for Social Research
The University of Michigan
Ann Arbor, Michigan

Institute for Energy Studies
Stanford, California

Institute of Nuclear Power
   Operations
1100 Circle 75 Parkway
Suite 1500
Atlanta, GA   30339

John Wiley, and Sons
605 Third Avenue
New York, NY   10158

The Journal of Energy and
   Development
International Research Center
   for Energy and Economics
216 Economics Bldg.
University of Colorado
Boulder, CO   80309

The Journal of Gulf and Arab
   Peninsula Studies
Post Office Box 17073
Shuaikh, Kuwait

Journal of Human Resources
University of Wisconsin Press
   Journals Division
114 N. Murray Street
Madison, WI   53715

Kennikat Press
New York, NY

Kramer Associates, Inc.
Washington, D.C.   20585

Kuwait Foundation for Advancement
   of Sciences
P.O. Box 25263
Safat, Kuwait

Kuwait Institute for Scientific
   Research
Post Office Box 24885
Safat, Kuwait

Marcel Dekker
270 Madison Avenue
New York, NY   10016

McClain Printing Company
212 Main Street
Parsons, WV   26287

Mid-Peninsula Conversion Project
867 West Dana, Suite 203
Mountain View, CA   94041

Monthly Labor Review
   Government Printing Office
Superintendent of Documents
710 North Capital Street, N.W.
Washington, D.C.   20402

Mountain West Research, Inc.
Room 306A, Fratt Bldg.
Billings, Montana 59101

Moving On
New American Research Institute
1300 West Belmont
Chicago, IL   60657

National Petroleum Council
1899 L Street, N.W.
Suite 1000
Washington, D.C.   20005

The National Planning Association
1606 New Hampshire Avenue, N.W.
Washington, D.C.   20009

National Productivity Council
Lodi Road
New Delhi, India   110003

National Science Foundation
   Research Applied to
   National Needs
1800 G Street, N.W.
Washington, D.C.   20550

National Technical
   Information Service
5285 Port Royal Road
Springfield, VA   22161

Oak Ridge Associated
   Universities
Post Office Box 117
Oak Ridge, TN   80401

OAPEC Bulletin
Organization of Arab Petroleum
   Exporting Countries
Post Office Box 20501
Safat, Kuwait

Oil and Arab Cooperation
OAPEC
Post Office Box 20501
Kuwait

Oil, Chemical, and Atomic
   Workers International
1636 Champs Street
Denver, Colorado 80201

OPEC Review
Pergamon Press, Inc.
Maxwell House, Fairview Park
Elmsford, NY 10523

Organization for Economic
   Cooperation and Development
International Energy Agency
2, Rue Andre - Pascal
75 775 PARIS CEDEX 16, France

Organization of Arab Petroleum
Post Office Box 20501
Safat, Kuwait

Pennsylvania State University
University Park, PA 16802

Pergamon Press Limited, Inc.
Maxwell House, Fairview Park
Elmsford, NY 10523

Plenum Press
233 Spring Street
New York, NY 10013

Preager Publishers
521 Fifth Avenue
New York, NY 10175

Review of Economics and Statistics
North-Holland Publishing Co.
Box 211
1000 AE Amsterdam, Netherlands

Rural Sociology
The Rural Sociology Society
325 Morgan Hall
University of Tennessee
Knoxville, TN 37916

Science
American Association for the
   Advancement of Science
1515 Massachusetts Avenue, N.W.
Washington, D.C. 20005

Solar Age
Solar Vision, Inc.
Church Hill
Harrisville, NH 03540

Solar Energy Information Services
600 East Tiffin
Post Office Box 600
Bascom, OH 44809

Solar Energy Research Institute
1536 Cole Blvd.
Golden, CO 80401

St. Martin's Press
175 Fifth Avenue
New York, NY 10010

Stanford Research Institute
Menlo Park, CA 94025

State of California
Employment Development Program
800 Capitol Mall
Sacramento, CA 95814

Sun Times
Solar Lobby
1001 Connecticut Ave., N.W.
Suite 510
Washington, D.C. 20036

Technology Review
Massachusetts Institute of
   Technology
Alumni Association
Cambridge, MA 02139

Texas Energy and Mineral
   Resources
Texas A & M University
College Station, TX 77843

Time, Inc.
10880 Wilshire Blvd.
Los Angeles, CA 90024-4193

TIMS Studies in Management
   Sciences
North-Holland Publishing Company
Box 211
1000 AE Amsterdam, Netherlands

U.K. Department of Employment
London, England

United Mine Workers' Journal
900 Fifteenth Street, N.W.
Washington, D.C. 20005

United Nations
Publishing Division
New York, NY 10017

United Nations Economic
   Commission for Western Asia
Mohamed Said Al-Altar
Post Office Box 27
Baghdad, Iraq

University of America Press
Post Office Box 19101
Washington, D.C. 20036

The University of Mississippi
Center for Manpower Studies
University, Mississippi

The University of Tennessee Press
293 Communications Bldg.
Knoxville, TN 37996

University of Toronto Press
33 East Tupper Street
Buffalo, NY 14203

The Urban Institute
2100 M. Street, N.W.
Washington, D.C. 20037

U. S. Department of Energy
Gov. Printing Office/NTIS
Superintendent of Documents
710 North Capital St., N.W.
Washington, D.C. 20402

U. S. Department of Health,
   Education and Welfare
Government Printing Office/NTIS
Superintendent of Documents
710 North Capital St., N.W.
Washington, D.C. 20402

U.S. Department of Labor
Government Printing Office
Superintendent of Documents
710 North Capital St., N.W.
Washington, D.C. 20402

U.S. Energy Research and
   Development Administration
Government Printing Office/NTIS
Superintendent of Documents
710 North Capital St., N.W.
Washington, D.C. 20402

Vantage Press
516 West 34th Street
New York, NY 10001

The Wall Street Journal
420 Lexington Avenue
New York, NY 10170

World Development
Pergamon Press, Inc.
Maxwell House, Fairview Park
Elmsford, NY 10523

Yale University Press
302 Temple St.
New Haven, CT 06520

Author Index

Includes authors and co-authors.
Numbers refer to citation entries, not page numbers.

A

Abo Saffara, Hassan 1
Ackermann, G. 163
Ahmad, Yusuf J. 164
Ahuja, Y. L. 32
Al-Abbas, Kasema A. 165
Al-Ali, Hashim M. 2
Al-Essa, Johayna S. 129
Al-Kamer, Jaseem 33
Al-Moussa, Ali 3
Allen, Edward L. 4, 18
Alleyne, D. H. N. 166
American Nuclear Society 34
Anderson, Marion 243
Andrews, John 35
Ansell, Jim 208
Arab Labor Organization 36, 130,
  167, 168
Arab Petroleum Training Institute
  36
Armington, Keith 175, 266
Armstrong, Richard 186
Arora, S. C. 169
Asian Development Bank 170
Aviel, David S. 131

B

Badre, Albert Y. 171
Bailey, James E. 96
Baker, Joe G. 37, 38, 132
Barany, Ronald 109, 255
Baratz, Morton S. 238

Barber, Sharla 85
Barker, Helen 172
Barker, Larry 43
Barnett, Samuel C. 208
Baron, C. 133
Baron, Thomas 39
Baroudi, Nouhad 40
Batelle Columbus Laboratories 41
Becker, David L. 173
Bell, Sharon E. 189, 244
Berg, Mark R. 5
Berndt, Ernst R. 6
Bernstein, Alan 252
Bezdek, Roger H. 97, 98
Bhutani, N. S. 169
Blair, L. M. 42, 43, 174
Bocock, Peter 51
Boroush, Mark A. 5
Boyet, W. E. 84
Brauer, Dieter 245
Brock, H. W. 44
Brodrick, J. 144
Brookes, L. G. 45
Brokes, W. 99
Brown, Robert 46
Buck, Neal A. 81
Buchsbaum, Steven 47
Bullard, Clark W. 7
Bungay, Henry R. 246
Burns, Barbara 175
Byer, Trevor A. 14

DJEHANE A. HOSNI is Assistant Professor of Economics at the University of Central Florida (U.C.F.), Orlando. Her interest in manpower development extends beyond the U.S. labor market to include the economies of the third world countries. She has several publications in manpower program evaluation (CETA), human resources development (Kuwait), and energy manpower planning (Arab World). She co-authored <u>United States Employment and Training Programs: A Selected Annotated Bibliography</u>.